W9-ANR-184

WILLS

A Do-It-Yourself Guide

Authors: Theresa Meehan Rudy and Jean Dimeo
Staff Review: Kay Ostberg
Additional Research & Writing: Curtis Washburn
Editor: Mary Collins
Graphics and Production: Scott Ward

Our thanks to the following consumer specialists and attorneys for their invaluable comments and advice: Jules Fink, Jack N. Hill, Winnie Huston, Leonard Kopelman, Herman Max Leibowitz, Caleen Norrod, Jerome Papania, Lawrence W. Waggoner, and Gregory Wilcox.

The original version of Appendix I, "State Laws Relating To Wills," first appeared in *Prepare Your Own Will, The National Will Kit*, by Daniel Sitarz, Nova Publishing, 1991.

First Edition: July, 1992

ISBN 0-910073-16-3

Also by HALT:

Using a Lawyer

Probate

Real Estate

Small Claims Court

Everyday Contracts

Trusts

Using the Law Library

Court & Judges

If You Want to Sue a Lawyer ...
A Directory of Legal Malpractice Attorneys

CONTENTS

PART IV – DRAFTING YOUR WILL

APPENDICES

INTRODUCTION

When someone dies in a novel or movie they always seem to have a last will and testament. Whole sagas evolve around who gets what and who disinherits whom. But in real life less than 30 percent of adult Americans have a will when they die. You don't have to be rich, famous or even on your death bed to have a will. All you need is children you care about or material possessions of some value – family photos, jewelry, a cherished heirloom – that you want to pass along to others.

If you die without a will, you lose control over who gets your property and who looks after your loved ones. Even if you think you have another 50 years in store, write your will now. You'll find it's easy, inexpensive and even fun to do.

HALT's step-by-step manual will show you how to create a legally valid will, without a lawyer, in all 50 states and the District of Columbia. This book explains what a will can do for you, how a will can work together with other estate planning tools – such as trusts – to save on taxes and estate settlement costs, and gives you the information you need to work knowledgeably with an estate-planning professional should you decide extra help is needed.

After reading this book you may decide, as thousands of Americans have in recent years, that you would like to set up a trust as a part of your estate plan. If you wish to investigate this option more closely, read HALT's book, *How to Use Trusts to Avoid Probate & Taxes.*

A Word About Terms

You shouldn't need a law degree to understand a will. Yet a discussion of wills can hardly occur without using some "legalese," such as *testator, executor, per stirpes* and *bequest.* Anyone who wants to draft a will or communicate their needs to an estate-planning professional must become familiar with these terms.

Every time a new legal term is used in this book, it's printed in *italics* and followed by a plain-language definition. There's also a glossary of legal terms that can be referenced at any time in Appendix VI.

You'll notice that the simple will in this book uses legal jargon only when absolutely necessary.

How To Use This Manual

Before you begin drafting your will, read through this book once and review the specific laws for your state. (See Appendix I.)

Part I of this book outlines the requirements for a legal will, explains what happens if you die without one, and underscores the importance of a complete estate plan.

Part II explains what property can or cannot be transferred through a will. It also provides guidelines for choosing an *executor* (the person who guides your will through estate settlement – called *probate*), discusses issues concerning your *beneficiaries* (those that inherit your property), and how to make a *bequest* (leave property). The section ends with a discussion of the different types of taxes you might owe and how to reduce them.

Part III contains the basic clauses you will use to draft your simple will. Part IV takes you through the steps to draft a will or, if necessary, to update a will. Appendices at the back of the book provide additional information.

Doing It Yourself vs. Using Professionals

Most people don't need a lawyer to draft a will if their distribution plans are simple. But, if after reading this book you decide that you do want professional assistance, study the low-cost options discussed in Chapter 10, including when to use a legal clinic, legal service plan or paralegal.

PART I

WILLS AND ESTATE PLANNING

Chapter 1:

ABOUT WILLS

The number one reason for writing a will is to leave instructions on how to distribute property. But a will can do a lot more than just that; it also allows you to:

- Name a *guardian* for minor children.
- Name an *executor* to distribute your property.
- Disinherit potential *heirs* (people who could inherit from you).
- Pay taxes owed on your *estate* (everything you own) as you instruct.

This chapter discusses some of the less familiar functions of a will.

Naming a Guardian

If you have minor children who are alive when you die, their other parent (your spouse, former spouse or non-marital partner) automatically becomes their guardian. But if both parents should die simultaneously, the picture becomes much cloudier. Wills provide protection against such disasters by giving you the opportunity to name a guardian for your children.

If your will names a guardian, you can be assured that your youngsters will be raised by someone you trust. Even though the court has the ultimate authority to appoint a guardian, it rarely rejects the parents' choice. If you do not choose a guardian before you die, the court will decide for you. It has full authority to ignore the advice of your friends and relatives, which means your child could end up with someone you wouldn't have chosen.

An example of a potential mix-up:

Example

Tom and Beth are a married couple in their mid-30s without wills who just had their first child. They would like their friends Teri and Andy to be their son's guardian. But when Tom and Beth are killed in a plane crash, the court gives custody of their boy to Tom's brother, even though Teri and Andy explain to the judge that the couple asked them to be the child's guardian.

A will is the only estate-planning tool that allows you to name a guardian to raise and educate your children. You and your spouse (or the child's other parent) should name the same guardian in your separate wills to avoid confusion about who gets guardianship.

Most people choose one person or couple to serve as both the personal and property guardian. For example, your sister Maria and brother-in-law Domingo may be loving parents and good money managers and could take care of all your children's emotional and financial needs.

Sometimes people choose two guardians – one to take care of the child's finances and another to care for the child. A "personal" guardian is responsible for the care, custody and upbringing of a child. A "property" guardian manages the youngster's inheritance until he or she reaches an adult age. Even if you think your kids are old enough to manage their own finances, minors can't legally own real estate or personal property worth more than $2,500 to $5,000, depending on which state you live in.

Some people ask a relative or friend to serve as the personal guardian and a bank to serve as the property guardian in order to invest and manage the child's inheritance. If you're thinking of this option, remember a bank will charge a hefty fee to manage the property. What's more, a bank is unlikely to have the personal ties that would make them go the extra mile to protect your child's interests. In the ever-changing financial world, you never know who could end up managing your child's finances – even if you entrusted the money to bank officials you know. Who knows who will own the bank when your child reaches adulthood?

Naming an Executor

A will can also be used to appoint the executor for your estate. The executor (sometimes referred to as a *personal representative* or *PR*) is responsible for settling your estate through probate. That involves collecting and inventorying your property, paying any debts and taxes owed, and supervising the distribution of your possessions. Some states exempt from probate estates with net values under a certain dollar limit – usually $10,000 to $60,000 – or estates that pass directly to a surviving spouse. Even if you think your estate will be exempt from probate, you still need a will that appoints someone to make sure your property is distributed as you direct. For information on executors, see Chapter 6.

Disinheriting Potential Heirs

You can disinherit anyone you want, except your spouse in most states and children under the age of 25 in Louisiana. You simply leave their name out of your will or include a clause that expressly disinherits them.

Chapter 7 explains more about your rights to disinherit.

Paying Taxes

You may be able to escape paying taxes when you die but your estate can't. If any state or federal estate and gift taxes (commonly referred to as *death taxes*) are owed, your executor needs to find the money in your estate to meet that obligation. A will allows you to identify which of your assets, or where in your estate, money for taxes should come from.

As you'll see in Chapter 9, however, most people don't have to worry about death taxes at all or, if they do, the amount they have to pay is minimal. If you do owe these taxes, and your will is silent on how they should be paid, your executor will have to rely on state laws for direction. Some states provide that death taxes are to be paid out of your *residuary estate* (what's left over after certain property has been distributed to your beneficiaries in accordance with your will); others provide that taxes should be paid proportionally by those who inherit from you. In those states, people who inherit could be forced to sell some or all of their inheritance just to help pay your taxes.

The will in this book prevents that from happening by allowing you to pay death taxes out of your residuary estate.

Chapter 2

IF YOU DIE WITHOUT A WILL

You may think you don't need a will. You're young and healthy and you can't imagine dying until the ripe old age of 92. Or you're elderly and single with a small house and only a few thousand dollars in savings. No matter what your age or financial status, you should have a will. Here's why.

Example

Mary, 57, and Brian, 58, are a childless couple who own a house, but have no wills. They separate and file for a divorce. Mary is killed in a car accident before the divorce is final. The state law gives all her possessions to Brian, who is still legally her husband, even though Mary wanted most of her things to go to her sister Geraldine.

Example

Scott and Diana, a married couple in their 20s, have a son, Danny, and no wills. They've talked about naming Scott's father as Danny's guardian, but have done nothing about it. When the couple is killed in a boating accident, the probate court appoints Diana's mother as Danny's guardian.

Example

Dennis and Mike have lived together for 10 years, but have never drawn up wills. When Mike dies of AIDS, the state law provides that Mike's possessions go to his parents and sisters, even though Mike would have preferred to have his property go to Dennis.

As these examples illustrate, state laws decide who gets your property when you die without a will – no matter what your relatives and friends tell the judge.

Surveys show that a majority of Americans die without a will (known as *intestate*). If you die intestate, the local probate court appoints someone – usually one of your family members – to collect and distribute your assets strictly by your state's intestacy laws. Your spouse, next-of-kin, friend or creditor can ask the probate court to appoint him or her as your estate's "administrator." But if none of your relatives, friends or creditors want the job or the court doesn't want to appoint them, the judge may appoint a court official, lawyer or banker to take your estate through probate and distribute your assets. If that happens, these professionals may charge your estate hefty fees for their services.

Each state has its own intestacy laws and procedures. The intestacy laws that apply to you are the laws where you legally resided. If you owned land in another state, the intestacy laws of that state may govern the distribution of that property. The entire process can be time-consuming and costly. First, there must be an official search for a valid will, even if everyone knows you didn't have one. When no will is found, an administrator must be appointed and often has to buy a *surety bond*. (A surety bond is a type of insurance that protects your estate and beneficiaries if the administrator mismanages your estate.)

If you're married and live in a community property state, everything you own goes to your spouse, unless your will requests otherwise. In common law (or separate property) states, some property goes to your spouse but other items can be divided among parents, siblings, and/or grandparents, depending on your state's law. (See Chapter 5 for more information on community property and separate property states.)

If you die intestate and don't have a spouse, children or other relatives who can be located, your estate is said to "escheat" and all your property reverts to the state you live in.

Chapter 3:

ESTATE-PLANNING TOOLS

Many people assume that only the wealthy need to worry about estate planning. In fact, estate planning should be considered by anyone who has anything they wish to pass on, loved ones they need to provide for after their death or personal health issues they need to consider. An estate plan can:

- Provide instruction on how others should handle your financial and medical decisions, if ever needed.
- Describe the burial arrangement you want.
- Designate who will inherit your property.
- Arrange for the care of your dependents.
- Minimize taxes and legal fees to be paid by your estate.

While a will is certainly a good first step, and a very important part of any estate plan, there are other planning tools you should know about. This chapter introduces you to those tools.

Estate-Planning Tools That Complement Wills

Three estate-planning tools are commonly used with wills: *testamentary trusts, durable powers of attorney for health care,* and *living wills.* This section explains what these tools do and discusses why you may want to draft one or more of them. It also discusses the importance of making any burial or organ donation wishes known before you die, how best to do that, and why a will is not the best place to share that information.

Testamentary Trusts

A testamentary trust, also known as a will-trust, allows your property to be managed or held for the benefit of family members and other beneficiaries long after you die. Unlike a will, which disposes of your property immediately after your death, a testamentary trust can be set up to support a dependent spouse or minor children, care for a disabled relative, educate a favorite niece, or do whatever you instruct it to do. Since the trust is created in your will, it will not go into effect until you die and until your will has been probated. (Trusts that avoid probate are discussed later in this chapter.)

To create a testamentary trust, you simply draft a will that meets the execution requirements for your state and include a clause that creates the trust. The trust clause will identify the person managing the trust (*trustee*), the person benefiting from the trust (*beneficiary*) and the property placed in the trust (*principal*). Chapter 11 of this book includes the necessary clause language to set up a testamentary trust for minor children. If you are interested in setting up a trust for a spouse or for a child with special needs, you should consult an estate-planning professional.

Durable Power of Attorney

You may want to appoint someone you trust to be your "health-care proxy" or "health-care agent" through a durable power of attorney for health care (DPAHC). A DPAHC is a document that allows you to name someone to make medical decisions for you if you lose the ability to make those decisions for yourself. You don't need to be deathly ill – you could be temporarily set back by an illness or injury and need someone to communicate your desires. Your incapacity, which is usually determined by one or more doctors, will trigger the DPAHC.

State laws regulating the powers given to a health-care proxy vary. Sometimes the person you've appointed can make all your medical decisions for you. In other instances, they can only consent to or refuse certain medical treatment. As long as you're mentally competent, you can revoke your DPAHC at any time. If you take a turn for the worse, your DPAHC can express your wishes with respect to being kept alive by artificial life-support systems (See "Living Wills" below) and in some states, it can also mention any organ donation wishes you make.

A separate durable power of attorney can be created to allow someone to manage your financial affairs during an illness or other incapacitation (a few states allow the person appointed to make both medical and financial decisions).

Living Wills

The right-to-die debate has pushed many dramatic stories about people subsisting on artificial life support into the headlines. Given the choice, most of us would prefer to die a natural death. You can take an important step toward that goal with a living will (also called a *directive* or *declaration*), which instructs your doctors and others about the use, withholding or withdrawal of artificial life-support systems when you become incapacitated or terminally ill and unable to communicate directions about what you want.

For more information on living wills and DPAHCs, refer to Appendix VII (Bibliography) and Appendix V (Sample Living Will). You can also obtain free state-specific forms on living wills and DPAHCs from *Choice In Dying*, 200 Varick Street, New York, N.Y. 10014.

Burial Wishes and Organ Donations

Since most wills are not read by family members until after funeral arrangements are made, it's advisable not to leave directions about burial and organ donations in a will. Instead draft a separate letter (or include the information in your "Letter of Instruction" discussed in Chapter 6) that explains what you want done. Include information on the type of ceremony or memorial service you want – religious or lay – whether you want to be buried, cremated, have your body donated to science, or organs donated for transplant. Also provide the name and location of a funeral home, information about the cemetery plot, and so on. Make sure your executor receives a copy of this letter before you die.

To donate specific organs or tissues to medical science or for transplants, you need to sign a "Uniform Donor Card" and carry it with you. Donor cards are available from the United Network for Organ Sharing (1-800-24-Donor) and other sources. Also, the motor-vehicle registration offices in 48 states offer a donor label that can be affixed to the back of your driver's license. If you change your mind about donating organs, just rip up your donor card or peel the label off of your driver's license or update your DPAHC.

Estate-Planning Tools That Avoid Probate

Any property you pass through a will must go through probate which is the legal process of settling your estate. It's often expensive and time-consuming and can involve lawyers and court appearances. If one of your goals is to avoid or minimize the effects of probate, you do have some options. You can:

- Set up a living trust.
- Name beneficiaries on insurance or re-tirement fund registration forms.
- Set up joint tenancy with a right of sur-vivorship on ownership documents, such as a bank account registration or the deed to real estate.

- Make outright gifts of property to your
  heirs while you're still alive.

All of these allow you to pass your property
directly to others without the need for probate.

Setting Up A Living Trust

The hottest estate-planning tool on the market
right now is the living trust — a document created
to take effect during a person's lifetime. In recent
years, these documents have become popular with
middle-income individuals and married couples
who want income from their money, but also want
to save their assets from the expense and delays of
probate after they die.

Most people who set up living trusts appoint
themselves (and, if they're married, their spouse)
as both *trustee* and income beneficiary. (A *trustee*
is the person responsible for managing the
property and assets in the trust, and for
distributing any income generated by the trust.)
Being trustee allows you to manage the trust and
to be paid by it when you want. After you die, the
remaining income and principal (i.e. the original
assets or property that was put into the trust) go
directly to the beneficiaries as you have instructed
in the trust.

Typically, if a married couple creates a living
trust and one of them dies, the trust becomes
irrevocable (unchangeable). The surviving spouse
continues to serve as trustee and continues to
receive income from the trust for life. After both
spouses die, their successor trustee (named in the
trust or by the court) steps in to keep the trust
going or to disburse its assets to the named
beneficiaries.

The major benefit of a living trust is that the
property placed in it isn't considered part of your
probate estate and therefore bypasses probate.
Another benefit is the amount of control and
flexibility living trusts can give you over your

property. You can create a living trust that is either revocable (meaning you can change or revoke it at anytime) or irrevocable (you can't change any of the terms of the document after you've signed it). The former gives you total control over what happens to the trust property while you're alive. The latter takes control away but rewards you with potentially large tax savings.

Naming a Beneficiary

Most retirement funds and all life insurance proceeds can be transferred directly to your beneficiaries without going through probate. When a beneficiary isn't named or is named but does not survive you, the proceeds become a part of your estate and are probated.

Individual Retirement Accounts

An Individual Retirement Account (IRA) is exempt from probate as long as you designate a beneficiary on the account registration document. However, the funds will have to go through probate if you name your estate as the beneficiary or your beneficiary dies before you do.

IRAs are particularly appealing because you can deposit up to $2,000 each year tax-free and save for your retirement. (There are some exceptions. You and your spouse must be covered by a qualified retirement plan and your combined income can't exceed certain IRS levels.) When you're finally ready to tap the account for cash, you will have to pay taxes on any previously untaxed amounts. You'll probably move into a lower tax bracket when you retire, so you'll still save money.

Keoghs

A Keogh is a retirement plan available for the self-employed. Like an IRA, if your Keogh account still contains money when you die, those funds will be released to the beneficiary you named on the account. The same exceptions apply. Taxes are also deferred on money invested in a Keogh until you make a withdrawal and, depending on your plan, you can invest as much as 25 percent of your income or up to $30,000, whichever is less.

Employer Pension Plans

If you are covered by a pension plan where you work, the benefits will only be paid out if you have a surviving spouse. Pension plans rarely pay benefits to anyone other than a spouse and are not considered part of the probate estate.

Life Insurance

Most Americans think of life insurance as a way to provide economic protection for those they love. According to the American Council of Life Insurance, nine out of 10 families have some kind of policy. ("Term" insurance covers you for a specific period and must be renewed for coverage to continue; you can't borrow against it. "Whole life" covers you until you die; you can cash it in for its accumulated value or leave the entire amount for your beneficiary to collect.)

As long as you list a beneficiary on your policy, the proceeds won't become part of your probate estate, though they will be considered part of your taxable estate. (See Chapter 9.)

Joint Tenancy with Right of Survivorship

People often share ownership of property through *joint tenancy with a right of survivorship* (JTWROS). Each owner (called a joint tenant) owns an equal and indivisible share of the property – whether it's stock, a residence or a savings account. When one joint tenant dies, his or her share automatically transfers to the surviving joint tenant(s) without passing through probate.

You can't give your joint-tenancy rights to another person in a will or testamentary trust because the surviving joint-tenants get your share when you die. To make sure you have an automatic right of survivorship, it's best to include a survivorship clause right on the ownership documents. If the ownership documents don't include such a clause, you can simply write the words "joint tenants with right of survivorship," after each name on the account registration or other ownership document, and make sure the information is recorded with any agency that needs to know about it (i.e., your bank, the recorder of deeds, and so on.)

Most estate-planning professionals feel that joint tenancy is an excellent arrangement for anyone who knows who they want their property to go to after they die. However, while it's true that you'll avoid probate by using JTWROS, the property will have to go through probate when the last surviving joint tenant dies.

Outright Gifts

If your estate is worth more than $600,000, your estate will probably have to pay a federal estate tax. But you can reduce your taxes by giving some of your money or other assets to your heirs during your lifetime. This is a common strategy for couples who intend to leave their children all of their property.

Under the *annual gift tax exclusion law*, an individual can give up to and including $10,000 a year, or a husband and wife can together make a gift of up to and including $20,000 a year, to each of any number of people, tax-free. The recipient (for example, your friend, relative or anyone else you have in mind) must have access to the gift immediately. It cannot be tied to some future event, such as reaching a specific age. If you want to give a gift with "strings attached" and still reduce your estate taxes, you must set up an irrevocable living trust.

In Conclusion

As you can see, estate planning involves more than just answering the question, "Who will get my property?" You also have to consider how that property can best be distributed to save time and taxes as well as the financial and personal needs of your children and potentially troublesome health-care decisions.

Chapter 4:

LEGAL WILLS

When most people think of a will, they picture a typewritten document filled with many legal terms that's signed in front of lots of people at a very solemn occasion. While it's true that wills need to be executed in a very specific manner, this stereotype doesn't quite provide a complete picture.

Witnessed wills are the most common type of will because they are legal in all 50 states and the District of Columbia; however, several states also recognize as legal an oral, handwritten, fill-in-the blank or joint will.

This chapter describes the legal requirements for executing different types of wills. The requirements for executing a Louisiana will differ from all other states and are covered later in this chapter and in greater detail in Chapter 14.

Types of Wills
Witnessed

Witnessed wills have a well-deserved popularity. They are valid in every state, can be changed (revoked) at any time until your death, can be tailored to meet your specific needs, and are the most likely to be accepted by a probate court as a valid expression of your wishes.

Witnessed wills, as their name suggests, are signed by people who witnessed you signing the will. Witnessed wills are usually typed documents, but they can also be handwritten. Generally they contain clauses that:

- Identify you as the will's maker (known as the *testator*).
- Appoint your primary executor and alternate executors.

- Appoint guardians for your minor children.
- Distribute specific gifts.
- Distribute your residuary estate (what's left over after specific and cash gifts have been given out).
- Provide for payment of any taxes owed, as you instruct.

Witnessed wills also can include clauses that forgive debts, disinherit children or other relatives, set up trusts, and even provide for orphaned pets.

In order to be valid, a witnessed will must be signed by you in front of two or three witnesses (depending on state laws,) who are not beneficiaries under the will and who know that the document they are witnessing is your will. It's not necessary to have a lawyer witness a will for it to be legal.

Fill-in-the-Blank (Statutory) Wills

California, Maine, Massachusetts, Michigan and Wisconsin have created statutory will forms that they sell for a nominal fee in legal stationery stores and from some probate courts. Statutory will forms are fill-in-the-blank printed forms that can be used by any married or single person who wants to draft an extremely simple will.

Most statutory will forms allow you to leave all your property to your spouse, or if your spouse isn't living, to your children. Generally, the forms have a provision that allows you to make just one other cash gift to whomever you choose. These will forms also have spaces for the name of your executor and alternate executor, the name of guardians for your minor children, and the signature of you and your witnesses.

Statutory will forms aren't suitable for anyone whose estate plan is even slightly more complicated than what was just described. You can't add or take out any provisions of the will, nor can you change the wording of any clause. So if you use a form, you won't be able to leave your silver pot to Aunt Reba, pass your cottage in Maine on to your cousin, or assign two guardians – one for finances and the other for care – of your kids.

Oral Wills

In most cases, oral (nuncupative) wills are only legal when used by active U.S. military personnel or Merchant Marines to distribute wages and personal property worth up to $1,000. They are invalid one year after the will's maker leaves the military or Merchant Marines. Some states allow others to make oral wills, but only if they're near death.

Like written wills, oral wills must be witnessed by at least two people, but the witnesses don't have to hear the words at the same time.

The two witnesses must swear that they heard the terms of your oral will directly from you. They must put the terms in writing and notify the surviving spouse and other possible heirs so they have the opportunity to challenge the validity of the will. People rarely create an oral will because they have no guarantee that their instructions will be carried out. It's usually a last minute option of a dying person who has no will.

Handwritten

Handwritten (holographic) wills, which are penned, dated and signed entirely by the person making the will, require no witnesses. Though they are valid in about a dozen states, probate courts are highly suspicious of them and will carefully examine the document to make sure it's in your handwriting. That process can really extend probate and may result in your will being thrown out.

Louisiana Wills

Louisiana's Napoleonic laws handle wills differently than any other state. The four recognized types in the state include mystic, oral, handwritten and statutory.

Mystic wills are typewritten documents that must have three witnesses, be notarized and sealed in an envelope.

There are two types of oral wills: public and private. Public oral wills are dictated to a notary who must handwrite the document. The will is then read aloud in front of the notary and three witnesses who reside in the same place where the will is being executed or by five witnesses if some reside outside of that area. If you choose to do a private oral will, you must write or dictate it and have it read aloud to you, a notary and five witnesses who reside in the place where the will is being executed, or seven if some live outside the region.

Louisiana also accepts handwritten wills as long as they are entirely written, signed and dated by you. They don't have to be witnessed. Like in other states, Louisiana courts carefully examine handwritten wills to make sure they're authentic. These wills can be thrown out as well.

Louisiana's statutory wills, not to be confused with the statutory will form mentioned before, are typewritten, witnessed and notarized documents. Louisiana residents can learn how to create a statutory will by using the clauses in this book and by following the special instructions that apply for their state in Chapter 14.

Joint Wills

A joint will is a typewritten will that's drafted by two people, usually a married couple. Each spouse must leave everything they own to the other. Then when the surviving spouse dies, the will provides instructions on how to distribute the property.

Few states recognize these wills. They're seldom used even where allowed because the will can't be changed after the death of the first spouse. So if your son has a child after your death, your spouse can't alter the will to include the new grandchild.

Video Wills

Hand-held video cameras may be the latest craze, but states still refuse to accept video wills as a valid will. Many people videotape a personal "will" for their family and friends to complement their typewritten will, but it's still an accessory, not the real thing.

Video wills can help substantiate your written will by proving that you were legally competent at the time you made your will. Some legal experts advise that you videotape the signing of your typewritten will to show that you were of sound mind and weren't being forced to sign the document.

Requirements of a Will

In order for a will to be legally valid, it must meet your state's technical requirements. (Louisiana residents should see page 122.)

Your will must:

- Either be typewritten, handwritten or oral (if the latter two types of wills are legal in your state). The simple will you'll create by using this book is typewritten. We recommend a typewritten will and explain more about preparing one in Chapter 14.
- Name you as the person writing the will.
- Be dated and signed by you.
- Be witnessed and signed by two or more people. The witnesses should be told that they're witnessing your will and they should be present at the time you sign the document.

Though it's not legally required, you should always name a primary and an alternate executor unless you don't care who the court appoints. Your will should also include at least one clause giving away property to one or more people or organizations. (However, courts have upheld as legal, wills that do not name executors or give away property – for example, a will that simply appoints a guardian for minor children is a valid will.)

In addition, *you* must meet a number of requirements as well. You must be:

- At least 18 years old when you sign your will. (In some states, you can be younger if you're married or in the military; in other states, you must be 21 years old. See Appendix I.)

- Of "sound mind," which means you know the people you've named as your beneficiaries and that you know the nature and extent of your assets. (Proof of insanity presented at the time a will is signed can lead the court to reject the will.)

PART II

BEFORE
WRITING A WILL

Chapter 5

YOUR PROPERTY

Most people draft a will to distribute property to family, friends and favorite charities. Before you decide what you want to leave to whom, you must know what is yours to give. This chapter describes property ownership laws and the legal limitations on giving away property through a will.

There are several ways you can own property. You can own property by yourself, jointly with others, or, if married, you may share what's known as "marital property" with a spouse (a discussion of how marital property can be distributed is included below.)

Once you familiarize yourself with this chapter, you can take the first step toward drafting your will by making a list of your property, what it's worth and to whom you want to leave it. (Appendix III includes a property inventory sheet.)

What You Can't Give Away In a Will

Usually property that cannot be left in a will is tied up in special arrangements geared towards keeping the property out of probate. Some examples include:

- Property owned by *joint tenancy with right of survivorship*. As discussed in Chapter 3, if you own property through a JTWROS, your co-tenant(s) automatically inherits your share after your death. Your share cannot be left to anyone other than the co-tenant(s).

- Property in *living trusts*. Property left in a living trust will automatically bypass probate because the trust owns the property, not you or your estate. The terms of your trust override your will.
- Property owned by *tenancy by the entirety*. This is a form of property ownership that some states have for married couples. It's almost identical to joint tenancy with right of survivorship except that the co-owners must be a married couple. They cannot dispose of property without each others' consent. When one spouse dies, the property automatically transfers to the surviving spouse and cannot be left in a will or trust to someone else.

The following "contractual" types of property also cannot be left in a will, but might still end up in probate if a surviving beneficiary isn't named on the contract form to receive the property. For example:

- Proceeds from a life insurance policy.
- Proceeds from a pension fund, IRA or Keogh.

What You Can Give Away In a Will

You can give away almost anything that you own. While that may seem simple enough, in fact there is a whole section of law called property law that is used to sort out who owns what. Basically, for the purposes of writing a will, there are three types of property you can give away: *separate property*, *tenancy in common property* or your share of *community property*. These are the only types of property you can give away in your will.

As its name infers, separate property is owned strictly by you and no one else. Married and unmarried couples may own separate property, but if you're married, chances are much of your property is jointly owned.

Example

Janet bought a new car before she and John were married. Since John never uses the car and the title is in Janet's name, the car is considered her separate property.

While this seems rather straight forward, property law gets more complex the more valuable a possession is. For most people, this means real estate ownership. While real estate is often "solely-owned," many people own houses or other *real property* with friends, relatives or business associates. The two most common ways of owning real estate are by joint tenancy with rights of survivorship (as mentioned above) and by tenancy in common. Tenancy in common means that you and your co-owners own shares in the real estate. Your co-owners have no claim to your share, which you can sell, put in a trust, or leave to someone in a will at your discretion. If the title doesn't say how you and your co-owners hold the property, most states consider you a tenant in common. (Don't let the word tenant mislead you; in this context tenant means co-owner, not renter.)

Community Property and Common Law Property

If you're married, the laws of your state will effect whether or not property is considered owned separately by you and, therefore, something you can give away in your will, or whether it's owned by you and your spouse and can't be given away.

Arizona, California, Idaho, Louisiana, Nevada, New Mexico, Texas, Washington, and Wisconsin are considered community property states; the rest are governed by common law.

Community Property States

In community property states, spouses are considered equal owners of all personal property and real estate acquired during marriage, even if only one spouse's name is on the deed or title. However, spouses can own separate property in community property states, including:

- Property owned before marriage, like a car, jewelry or clothing.
- Property received as a gift or inheritance before or during marriage.
- Income earned by property (except in Texas, Wisconsin and Idaho, where income from separate property is considered community property).
- Social Security and Railroad Retirement benefits.
- Most personal injury awards and settlements (check your state law to be sure).

Generally speaking, both spouses are liable for the debts of shared community property, but they are solely responsible for the debts of the separate property they own. For example, both Janet and John would be responsible for paying the mortgage on a jointly-owned home, but only Janet would pay her car loan since the car is in her name only.

In Louisiana, if the spouse who died was rich in relation to the surviving spouse, the survivor has a right to their half of the property plus:

- Another one-fourth of the estate if the couple doesn't have children.
- Lifetime use of another one-fourth until remarriage or if there are three or fewer kids.

- Lifetime use of a share equal to each
  child's share if there are four or more
  children. (See Appendix I for more
  information about Louisiana.)

When a married couple moves to a community
property state and brings property that was
acquired during marriage in a common law state,
that property is called quasi-community property.
When one spouse dies, the surviving spouse owns
only one-half of it, but for federal estate tax
purposes, quasi-community property is taxed as
separate property, not community property.

Common Law States

In states that do not have community property
laws, *common law* applies: The spouse whose
name is on the deed or title is considered the
property owner. If ownership is unclear at the
time of one spouse's death, the court will decide
who owns it by considering how much each
person paid for it, who took care of it, and who
used it.

In common law states, the property each spouse
owns separately includes everything:

- In your name only (the deed, title or other
  legal document says you're the owner).
- You have purchased separately with your
  own money.
- You have inherited or that was given to you
  as a gift and not mixed with property
  shared with your spouse.

Husbands and wives can give their separate
property to whomever they choose; the beneficiary
doesn't have to be the other spouse. But to protect a
spouse from being disinherited, common law
states give the survivor rights to one-third to one-
half of the deceased spouse's property (called the
spouse's minimum share). In West Virginia, the
spouse's share is calculated as a percentage of the

couple's combined property; in long term marriages (15 or more years), the spouse's share is 50 percent. A surviving spouse may choose to accept what was left in the will or to elect to get their state's statutory share. In order to calculate the surviving spouse's share, the state law may take into consideration whether any trusts and joint tenancy agreements were set up to try to defeat the spouse's rights.

Property Inventory

To figure out exactly what you can legally give away, you should prepare a property inventory that identifies what you own and how you own it. Your property inventory sheet should contain the following information:

- Identify your real estate.
- Identify your personal property.
- State the ownership arrangement of the property (i.e., JTWROS, tenancy by the entirety, tenancy in common, separate).
- State the percentage of the property that you own.
- Estimate the net value of your property.

A sample property inventory list can be found in Appendix III.

Chapter 6:

EXECUTORS

Choosing an executor may be the most important estate-planning decision you make. Once approved by the court, the person you've named in your will is legally responsible for taking your estate through probate – paying your bills and taxes and inventorying and distributing your property based on your instructions. If you die without a will, the court will appoint someone to handle these responsibilities. A judge may appoint your spouse, another relative or friend, but could just as easily appoint a local banker or lawyer who won't have any idea how you wanted your property distributed.

HALT hears all too frequently about probate "horror stories" where estates are drained for years by probate fees and expenses while the family stands by with little power to stop the waste. Obviously, it can't be emphasized enough – think carefully before choosing your executor.

Choosing Your Executor

We advise you to name someone you trust who is also personally interested in seeing your estate settled quickly and efficiently, such as one of your beneficiaries. Your executor doesn't have to be an accountant, attorney, or mathematical genius to successfully take your estate through probate and distribute your assets. If your will is properly drafted and your executor has access to your property, or at least information about its whereabouts, his or her job won't be difficult or overly time-consuming.

If it does become difficult, your executor can always hire an attorney or accountant to help settle the estate. It's much better to appoint someone interested in your estate as executor who has the ability to hire a lawyer than to appoint a lawyer as executor. While some jurisdictions require a lawyer's help during the probate process, your executor should be aware that laws regulating probate fees dictate only what a lawyer is *allowed* to charge, not what they're *required* to charge. So your executor can shop for a lawyer who might charge by the hour and only for work actually done.

Many people name their spouse, adult children or a close relative as their executor. This is a good idea because they will be more likely to settle an estate quickly and follow your wishes. If you don't have any close family members who could be the executor, a friend, business associate, family lawyer or banking institution can also perform the duties.

You're required by law to select someone who is 18 years or older, of sound mind and a U.S. citizen. It's practical to hire someone who lives in the same state as you, although it isn't a requirement in most states. And, unless you specifically waive the requirement in your will, any executor you name will have to post a surety bond (this could run twice the value of the debts of your estate) with your estate picking up the cost of the bond. In some states, even if you waive the bond requirement, the executor may be required to post a minimum bond to cover at least the estate's debts.

A bond is a type of insurance that provides some financial protection for your estate and beneficiaries if your executor steals from you or mismanages your estate. If you trust your executor, you can save time and money by waiving the requirement. It's wise to require a bond, however, if you have to rely on someone you don't know.

You should name at least one alternate executor in your will. That way, if your first choice is unavailable, your next choice can be appointed. If you don't name an alternate, the probate judge may have to choose one.

Using Co-Executors

One or more people can serve as executor. If you appoint co-executors, both must sign off on each step of probating your estate. You might name your two eldest children, or a spouse and one of your adult children, as co-executors. Perhaps your preferred executor lives out-of-state and you want to have a co-executor nearby.

If you are going to name two executors, it's a good idea to choose two people who can cooperate effectively in order to minimize conflicts. You can draft provisions to deal with potential disagreements between the co-executors, like providing that one has the right to override the other's decisions. Due to coordination problems, it's not advisable to name more than two people as co-executors. The clauses in this book allow you the option of appointing one executor or two.

The Executor's Responsibilities

The person you choose as executor should know in advance what will be expected of him or her and should agree to take on the job. While the job isn't difficult, it will take a substantial amount of time and may require several trips to court, visits with family members and consultations with any of a number of potentially interested parties – insurance agents, accountants, a family lawyer, banker or employer.

You can make your executor's job easier by including a clause in your will that grants your executor a wide-range of powers to handle all the responsibilities involved in settling your estate. That way they won't have to petition the probate court every time they need to make a quick decision or fulfill a routine obligation. If you fail to put this requirement in your will, the presiding judge or your state's laws may grant your executor more limited powers.

Powers typically granted to an executor in a will include the right to:

- Retain or collect property until it's distributed.
- Sell, invest, mortgage or lease property.
- Settle claims in favor of, or against, the estate.
- Pay creditors.
- Operate or close down any business.

The executor clause this book uses gives your executor broad powers. We recommend giving broad powers. If you don't, your executor will need court approval for most steps in the probate process, which can run-up costs and lengthen the time it takes to settle your estate. If you want to leave specific instructions about what your executor should or shouldn't do – for example, not sell the family home – write the details in a separate letter to your executor. (See the Letter of Instruction section later in this chapter.)

The Executor's Duties

Depending on the size of your estate, your executor will have to follow a simple or more formal process when taking your estate through probate. The duties required for settling an estate include:

- *Opening the Estate.* The executor begins the probate process by notifying the court, your beneficiaries and creditors of your death. The executor must file the original copy of your will and death certificate with the probate court in the county where you lived.

- *Inventorying the Property.* The executor
  needs to list the assets going through
  probate, including personal property,
  money in accounts, any share in real estate
  owned by tenancy in common, etc. (Jointly-
  owned property, pension plans, trust
  property and anything else that passes to
  beneficiaries outside of probate does not
  need to be included in this inventory.) The
  inventory must be filed with the court
  usually within three months.
- *Paying Creditors.* Creditors must file
  claims against your estate within the time
  limits required by law. If they fail to file on
  time, your estate is not legally obligated to
  pay that debt. If it were, your executor
  might have to wait a considerable length of
  time before settling your estate and
  distributing your assets. Your executor
  may be able to pay off some debts with
  money from a savings or checking account.
  Other larger debts may have to be paid out
  of your residuary estate.
- *Closing the Estate.* In cases where a final
  accounting is required, all that's needed is
  a simple balance sheet that shows the
  estate's assets.
- *Distributing the Estate.* In some states,
  once the final account and the closing
  papers have been filed, the executor must
  wait for the Registrar to complete an audit
  before the estate's assets can be distributed.

Plain-language state-specific guides on
executor duties may be available in bookstores or
through your probate court. Ask your executor to
check it out.

Paying Executors

Most state statutes entitle an executor to a fee, generally no more than three to five percent of the value of the estate.

If you choose a beneficiary or close friend as your executor, they'll probably waive a substantial portion, if not all, of the fee. But if you name a financial institution or lawyer as executor, they'll probably charge the maximum amount allowed by law. In some states, they can even collect a double fee – one for serving as executor and another for serving as the estate's lawyer.

Letter of Instruction

You can help your executor by writing an informal Letter of Instruction which typically includes information not found in your will. It's not legally binding, but does give an executor guidance. While it often includes a complete list of your assets and their whereabouts, you don't have to enclose that information if you've already given a copy of a complete personal inventory to your executor.

There may be many pieces of information you have that will help your executor settle your estate quickly and efficiently, such as the location of keys, the combination to your safe deposit box, the whereabouts of important papers or stored valuables. Your letter can also give your executor burial instructions or make your wishes known about organ donations.

Many people use their Letter of Instruction as an opportunity to say something personal to their family and friends. If you foresee some disputes among your beneficiaries concerning the distribution of your possessions, you may want to give your executor tips on how to settle those conflicts fairly.

Model Letter of Instruction

Dear Sarah,

Well, we knew it was only a matter of time given my recent illness before you'd be reading this letter. I've typed up a few notes that should help you get started. Hope everything goes smoothly, Sarah.

Some thoughts on what needs to be done before my funeral:

I've made burial arrangements with Farragher's Funeral Home (212/555-5555). The funeral director, Mr. Graves, will handle all the details. He knows that I prefer not to have a wake – a simple service will do just fine. You should know that I've already paid for my coffin and cemetery plot. The deed for my plot and receipts for my coffin are in the left hand drawer of the desk in my study at home.

You'll find the key to the desk drawer on the top shelf of the bookshelf in the study, behind the copy of Moby Dick. Make sure you hold onto that key because there are a number of other important documents in that desk drawer: my life insurance and IRA account papers, birth certificate, title to my car, and so on. The deed to my house and other really important papers are kept in a safe deposit box at 1st National Savings & Loan on Elm Street. Keys to that box and to my Post Office Box, #001, are in the desk drawer in the yellow and green envelope.

After things have settled down and the funeral is over, you'll have to submit my will for probate. It's already on file at the Probate Court downtown. The probate clerk should be able to fill you in on the next steps to take. It might help, however, if you bring my death certificate with you when you go to the court and a copy of my will to prove you're the executor. (You can get a copy of my will from that desk drawer, along with a complete inventory of everything I own and a list of important telephone numbers.) Once you find it, please make a copy for everyone mentioned in my will.

I've been told that the probate court distributes a handy step-by-step guide for executors. Perhaps the clerk's office will send out a copy if you call them. Their phone number is 212/555-5151.

Just between the two of us, I'm a little concerned that some of my kids will fight over my possessions. I hope it doesn't come to that, but if it does, remind them of the no will-contest clause I included in my will and your implicit right to enforce it.

I just want to end this letter by stating that I have every confidence our friendship doesn't end here. Until we meet again …

Love,

Susan

Chapter 7:

BENEFICIARIES

Most people are pretty clear about whom they want to leave property to in their will. This chapter discusses some things you should consider before making this decision.

You can use your will to give your property to anyone or any organization you choose with few exceptions – you can't completely disinherit a spouse and, if you're a Louisiana parent, you can't disinherit children under the age of 25.

Most people leave their possessions to close relatives and friends, but some also remember favorite schools, churches and other charities in their will. The person or organization you select to receive money or property from your will is called your beneficiary.

Typical Beneficiaries

The most common beneficiaries are family members, but only your surviving spouse has any legal right to part of your estate.

Spouses. It's illegal in nearly every state to disinherit a spouse unless they've signed a premarital or postmarital agreement forfeiting their rights to your property after you die. As mentioned in Chapter 5, a surviving spouse can reject the terms of your will and receive a percentage of your estate set by law (usually one-third to one-half). This "right of election" law was designed to prevent someone from leaving their spouse dependent on government aid.

If a surviving spouse chooses to exercise the right of election so they can get more of the estate, other beneficiaries may have to give up their inheritance. They may eventually be entitled to own the property that was given to the surviving spouse, but they can't take control of it or use it until the surviving spouse dies. Unless your spouse has agreed otherwise, plan to leave at least what they're entitled to inherit under your state's law. If you're considering giving anything less, and your spouse hasn't agreed to it, you need to consult an estate-planning professional.

Children and grandchildren. Offspring are typical beneficiaries even though they have no legal right to your estate (except in Louisiana, where biological and adopted children under the age of 25 usually can't be disinherited). Leaving an out-right inheritance in your will to a disabled child who is on government benefits, such as Supplemental Security Income (SSI), will, in all likelihood, jeopardize that child's right to receive public funds. Parents who wish to avoid this situation should consult a professional about their estate-planning options, such as disinheriting the child in their will and instead setting up a special-needs trust.

Non-relatives. Many people leave part or all of their estate to friends, neighbors, co-workers and "significant others." Often, unmarried couples create separate wills that leave everything to each other. If you want to leave your estate to a non-relative, and know that a family member will challenge that decision, you may want to create a trust instead. At the minimum, your will should include a clause that expressly disinherits anyone likely to contest your will.

Charitable Organizations. Favorite charities are frequently remembered in wills. Such philanthropy can also lower taxes for larger estates. If your primary reason for leaving money or property to charity is to save on taxes, the charity must qualify as a tax-exempt non-profit organization under the IRS's code section 501(c)(3). Most non-profits – such as the American Cancer Society, your church, your alma mater, HALT – qualify as tax-exempt charities. Gifts to them will be deducted from your gross estate before taxes are calculated.

If you have a large estate, instead of leaving money through your will, you may want to set up a charitable trust. Depending on the type of charitable trust you create, it can provide you with lifetime income from the assets you plan to donate, reduce the size of your taxable estate, and even give you a say in how the charity spends your money long after you have died. For more information about charitable trusts, see HALT's book, *How to Use Trusts to Avoid Probate and Taxes*.

Even though most states place no restrictions on gifts to charities once a spouse has been provided for, some do have limits or only honor gifts that a person put into their will more than a year before they died. Check Appendix I to see whether any restrictions apply.

Disinheriting

With the exception of a surviving spouse (and children in the state of Louisiana), you can disinherit anyone you want just by leaving his or her name out of your will. If you decide to disinherit a child – biological, adopted or stepchild – it's advisable to specifically mention your child's name in a disinheritance clause. That way a court will realize your true intention if your child contests on grounds that you simply forgot to mention his or her name in the will. In fact, if other relatives (or even non-relatives) are likely to challenge your will because they weren't named in it, it's wise to expressly disinherit them by name in your disinheritance clause.

Don't try to "get even" with the person you're disinheriting in your will by listing the reasons you dislike them. While that won't invalidate your will, it's unwise behavior since the shunned person may be able to sue your estate for libel (that is, for making inflammatory and public remarks about his or her reputation). On the other hand, if you're disinheriting a child because you already gave that child a lot more money than your other children while you were alive, it might be wise to give that reason in your will.

Naming Beneficiaries

This book allows you to name both a primary and alternate beneficiary for any property you want to leave in your will. Before you begin drafting, decide who you want to give your property to. The worksheet in Appendix III includes spaces for writing down the names of beneficiaries and spaces for identifying the property you plan to leave them.

If the first person you select (your primary beneficiary) dies before you or is otherwise unable to collect your property, an alternate (contingent) beneficiary can be named to receive that property, thereby speeding up the process of settling your estate.

To name beneficiaries in your will, you should identify them by their legal name – Elizabeth Cheever, not Beth Cheever. If your beneficiary has a common name like John Smith and isn't related to you, include a middle name and/or address as well. The same is true for naming charitable organizations – use their legal title, HALT/Americans for Legal Reform, not just HALT.

People You Should Not Name

Do not name any professional who helped you draft your will as one of your beneficiaries. The legal profession frowns upon lawyers who inherit from a will they helped prepared, because of the suspicion it raises – that you were somehow coerced into making the lawyer a beneficiary.

Anyone who witnessed your signing of the will shouldn't be named as a beneficiary because they are not supposed to have a stake in the will. Some states automatically reject a will that is witnessed by a beneficiary.

Establishing Survivorship

Most people include a survivorship clause in their will. This sets a time (usually 30 to 60 days) that your beneficiary must survive you in order to inherit under the terms of your will. You can safely pick any limit up to 180 days without slowing down the estate settling process because probate can take from six months to a year or more.

Without this clause, your property might be taxed twice and go through probate twice – first when you die and again when your beneficiary dies shortly after you. Without this clause, your beneficiary's heirs, not your alternate beneficiary, will inherit your property.

The survivorship clause used for the simple will created in this book is found in Chapter 11.

Marital Considerations

You should pay special attention to this section if you're separated or divorced.

Married but Separated

If you're married but legally separated from your spouse and neither of you have plans to file for divorce, you need a will that reflects your separation agreement. Even though you are technically still married, your separation agreement should state that it supersedes any rights your spouse might have under law to part of your property.

As long as the both of you still agree on the terms of your separation agreement, you can create a will leaving as much or as little of your property to your spouse as you want. If your spouse objects, or is likely to object, consult a professional before drafting your will.

Divorce

If you're divorced and have never written a will (or updated your will since marriage) you need to do so. As mentioned in Chapter 2, if you die without a will, your estate will be divided according to state intestacy laws – your children and parents will be the primary recipients of any property you leave behind. If your former spouse still co-owns property with you, it's probably under a tenancy-in-common arrangement whereby each of you can do what you please with your share of the property.

If you're divorced and die before updating your will, your state may revoke (cancel) any gift made in your will to your former spouse, but leave the rest of your will intact. Or, it may revoke your entire will. (See Appendix I.) Even so, as soon as your divorce becomes official, it's a good idea to draft a new will to make sure your property ends up in the hands of the people you want. The same applies to other documents, such as life insurance, IRAs, or a pension account.

Second Marriages

If you've been married more than once and have children from your previous marriage, your estate-planning needs may be more complex. You now have two families to consider when drafting your will. Many state laws protect your new spouse by entitling him or her to a certain percentage of your estate when you die regardless of your new spouse's wealth at the time or any children you have from a previous marriage. If you and your spouse can't agree on how to distribute property to children from a previous marriage, you should seek professional estate-planning help.

Chapter 8:

MAKING BEQUESTS

After figuring out what you own and whether or not you can leave it in your will, it's time to think about how to divvy up your property. This chapter describes how to make a bequest (that is, a gift left by will) to the people you've chosen as beneficiaries.

To simplify matters, this chapter refers to all gifts left in a will – whether real estate, personal property or money – as bequests. When you draft a will, you don't need to use the word bequest, nor do you need to use the words *legacy* or *devise*. (Gifts of money are often called legacies and gifts of real estate, such as a house or land, are called devises.)

You just need to be clear about what you're giving away. We explain how to describe gifts of money, personal property and real estate so that everyone involved understands exactly what you want to give away and whom you want to give it to. Additional ideas on how to describe gifts left by will can be gleaned from Appendix IV, which includes sample wills.

Types of Bequests

Estate planners talk about three kinds of bequests: specific, general and residuary. Basically, the difference between the three is whether you're leaving someone a specific item, a share of your estate to be paid out of your estate's general assets, or the leftovers – called residue – after specific and general bequests have been made. This book shows you how to make all three types of bequests.

Specific Bequests

If you want to leave something specific – such as a painting, a car, a piece of jewelry, a home, a vacant lot, stocks, bonds, or the balance on a checking or savings account – you need to make what is called a "specific bequest" in your will. Even if you want to leave a collection of items, such as "all my household furnishings," that, too, is considered a specific bequest.

Before you make any specific bequests, you need to ask yourself, "Will the item(s) I want to leave still be part of my estate when I die?" If the answer is "no," your beneficiary gets nothing. If specifically bequested property no longer exists at the time of your death because it was sold, or destroyed, the beneficiary has no right to collect from your estate. So, while you may think you have left a sizeable gift to your daughter by leaving her all your jewelry, if your gems are stolen in a burglary before you die and you haven't had a chance to update your will, she may get nothing – not even the insurance proceeds.

For this reason, you must be careful about making specific bequests. Many people who draft simple wills choose to limit the specific bequests they make to a few sentimental or particularly valuable items, if they make specific bequests at all.

This book allows you to make specific bequests out of your personal property (cash, cars, clothing, furniture, pictures, etc.) and out of your real property (house, condo, land, etc.). The will clauses that allow you to do this appear in Chapter 12. For each gift of real or personal property you make, you will describe the item you want to leave and you'll name a primary and, if desired, alternate beneficiary to receive it. If neither beneficiary collects, the item(s) becomes a part of your residuary estate.

Here is an example of a will clause that leaves personal property:

> I give my stereo equipment to Joan Kelly if she survives me, or if not, to Rex Blonden. If my alternate beneficiary does not survive me, I direct that my stereo equipment become a part of my residuary estate and distributed accordingly.

Here is an example of a will clause that leaves real property:

> I give the house and land located at 178 Orchard Street, Bethesda, MD, to Trinita Collins if she survives me, or if not, I direct that the house and land located at 178 Orchard Street, Bethesda, MD, become a part of my residuary estate and distributed accordingly.
>
> If the property identified above is subject to a mortgage, deed of trust, lien or other encumbrance at the time of my death, such encumbrances shall pass intact to the beneficiary receiving that property.

Describing Specific Bequests

The description of your specific bequest doesn't need to be lengthy, but it does need to be exact or you run the risk of confusing people about your intentions, or worse, making an invalid bequest.

If you plan to make a specific bequest of personal property, you should identify the item(s) clearly. The description can be quite simple, for example, my tool collection, my dining room set, all my clothing, my car (if you only have one vehicle). A simple description works well with some personal property because if you replace the item during your lifetime with something similar – an oak dining room set with a mahogany one – your beneficiary receives the dining room set you owned at the time of your death. If you're too specific, your beneficiary may or may not be able to collect.

Others personal possessions may need more elaboration, especially if you have more than one of the type of item you're giving away – my sapphire and diamond ring, my Zenith 25-inch color TV, my 1985 black Mercedes-Benz, etc.

If you plan to make a specific bequest of cash, stocks or bonds, you should identify where the gift is to come from, for example, a bank account, stock portfolio or other source, and you should include account numbers. For example, "I give $5,000 to Mairéad McDonough from Savings Account 123-456-7 at 1st National Bank ..." If the balance of the account you specify is lower than the amount of your specific bequest, your beneficiary might only receive the balance and not more. If the balance is higher, the difference will become part of your residuary estate. For accounting purposes, it's easier to bequest an entire account (or all your stocks or bonds) so that whatever the balance is at the time of your death, that is the amount your beneficiary will receive.

If you plan to make a specific bequest of real estate (real property), you should identify the property by its address, lot number or other identifier. You should also be clear about whether the property is entirely yours to give or if only a portion of it is yours to give. For example, if you co-own a house, you can't say, "I give the house and land located at 131 Main Street, ..." since you don't own the whole house to give. You must say, "I give my share of the house and land located at 131 Main Street,..." And, as in the example above involving the house at 178 Orchard Street, you should be clear that the property passes to your beneficiary subject to any encumbrances on it (mortgages, deed of trusts, liens). If you want real estate to pass free of all encumbrances, you must state that in your will and you must be sure that your estate is large enough to pay off the debts. You may want to consult a professional to be certain.

General Bequests

General bequests are primarily used to give away specific sums of money. You should make a general bequest if you care about the actual amount being given and don't want to worry about what may or may not be left in an account at the time of your death, and don't care what might need to be sold to leave money to a beneficiary.

All general bequests are paid out of your estate's general assets. When you bequest money, your executor has to fulfill the bequest even if it means selling some or all of your property. Before making large cash gifts under a general bequest clause, ask yourself, "Is there enough cash on hand or are my assets liquid enough (easily convertible to cash) to fulfill this bequest?" If the answer is no, think about whether you really want your home, car or other expensive item sold just so Uncle Finbarr can receive the $10,000 you've always wanted to give him.

If your estate doesn't have sufficient assets to fulfill the general bequests you want to make, some or all of your bequests may have to be reduced (*abated*). State laws typically require that the size of your residuary estate be reduced first, then your general cash bequests and finally, your specific bequests.

The fill-in-the-blank clause for a general bequest appears in Chapter 12. It allows you to describe the amount of cash you want to leave and to name a primary and alternate beneficiary. If neither collects, the cash becomes a part of your residuary estate.

Here's an example of a general bequest:

> I give the sum of $5,000 to Elois Butler if she survives me, or if not, to Georgie Montgomery. If my alternate beneficiary does not survive me, I direct that the sum of $5,000 become a part of my residuary estate and be distributed accordingly.

Residuary Bequests

Anything left in your estate after specific and general bequests are made and your debts and taxes are paid is called the "residue" of your estate. A residuary clause can be used to give away your entire estate (if *no* specific or general bequests have been made), the bulk of your estate (if only a few specific and/or general bequests have been made), or it can be used as a catch-all clause to distribute property inherited at the last minute or to distribute specific or general bequests that were not, for whatever reason, given out.

Estate planners strongly recommend using a residuary clause in your will, because it allows you to account for all of your property without having to specifically list each item. Since most people buy and get rid of property regularly, it makes sense to have this clause.

If you plan to leave your residuary estate to several people and/or to charitable institutions, it's best to give away your estate in percentages rather than designating specific sums of money. This way you distribute your assets in the proportions you want and save your executor the headache of deciding exactly who gets how much. You should also name an alternate beneficiary.

Here's an example of a residuary bequest:

> I give the residue of my estate, whether real or personal and wherever situated, in equal shares to John Vitkuske and Julie Vitkuske if they survive me. If either of my named beneficiaries do not survive me, than (his/her) share shall go to my surviving beneficiary. If both of my beneficiaries fail to survive me, than I give the residue of my estate to the American Lung Association.

Typically, people leave the residuary estate to their spouse as the primary beneficiary, with their children as the alternate beneficiaries and their grandchildren as the second alternates. If you're planning this distribution scheme, you should

know that there are two ways to pass your estate
on to your descendants – *per stirpes* or *per capita.*

Passing Property to Descendants

Under a per stirpes distribution plan, if one of
your children dies before you do, their share is
divided evenly between their kids. So for example,
if you left your estate in equal thirds to your three
adult children, but one child died before you, that
child's living *issue* (direct descendants; children,
grandchildren) would divide their parent's one-
third in equal shares.

Under per capita – another distribution scheme
for family members – if one of the named
beneficiaries in your will dies before you do, all of
your remaining named beneficiaries will inherit
the share that the deceased beneficiary would
have taken, equally. So, if you started with 10
named beneficiaries but only have nine living
when you die, each will inherit one-ninth of your
estate.

An example of a residuary clause with a per
stirpes distribution plan reads as follows:

> I give the residue of my estate, whether real or personal
> and wherever situated, to my dear wife Janet Bergen if
> she survives me. If she does not survive me, than I give
> the residue in equal shares; one to each of my children
> who survive me. If any of my children should not survive
> me, I give their share to their children or issue, if they
> have any, per stirpes.

Modifying Bequests

Up to this point we've described the different
types of bequests you can make and when you
might want to use them. This section shows you
how to alter specific, general and residuary
bequests to accommodate some personal needs you
might have.

While we don't recommend making lots of
changes to the bequest language presented in this

book, there's also no need to produce a sterile document that sounds cold or even callous. You're free to use terms of endearment – beloved, special, favorite; identify the relationship of the beneficiary to you – sister, brother, good neighbor; express appreciation – "for all the help you've given me"; or to express your wishes (not demands, though) about how a bequest should be used – for a college education, a new car.

Some of the ways you can modify a bequest are by:

• *Deleting alternate beneficiaries.* Note that in both the specific and general bequest clauses, you can appoint a primary and alternate beneficiary and, if either fail to receive your bequest, your residuary estate acts as the back-up "beneficiary." You may, however, have only one person in mind for a specific bequest. If that's the case, feel free to delete the alternate.

Here's how you'd write a specific bequest clause making two slight modifications: deleting an alternate *and* identifying the relationship of the beneficiary to you.

> I give my dining room set to my dear sister-in-law Linda Byrne if she survives me, or if not, I direct that my dining room set become a part of my residuary estate and be distributed accordingly.

You should *always* name an alternate beneficiary in your residuary estate clause, because it's your last chance for distributing property.

• *Add minor conditions or acknowledgements.* You can modify a bequest clause by stating how you'd like the bequest used or you can acknowledge why a bequest is being made. Here are two examples:

> I give the sum of $10,000 to my grandson Noah Plante to be used for his college education, if he survives me, or if not, I direct that the sum of $10,000 become a part of my residuary estate and distributed accordingly.

> I give $5,000 to my dear friend David O'Rourke for all the help he gave my father over the years, if he survives me, or if not, I direct that the $5,000 become a part of my residuary estate and distributed accordingly.

When placing a condition (also called a contingency) on how a bequest can be used, realize that you may be creating unforeseen problems for the named beneficiary. For example, what happens if grandson Noah doesn't want to go to college or has already finished college before you die? Does he get the $10,000 anyway or does the bequest fail? It's a judgment call for the executor and a possible lawsuit for your estate if the executor's answer is "no." If you try to place too many conditions on how or when a bequest can be fulfilled, you no longer have a "simple will" and your estate may take longer to settle. If you want to control how or when most of your property can be used, you're better off setting up a trust.

You cannot make a bequest conditional on an illegal action or on an action that courts consider goes against "public policy." For example: "I give the sum of $20,000 to Cammy Boggs to start a marijuana farm ..." If you do make a bequest contingent on an illegal condition or one that violates public policy, the court will ignore the bequest and may even void your entire will.

Chapter 9:

TAXES

The federal government and some states tax property passed to your beneficiaries after you die. The amount of this tax, called estate tax, is determined by your wealth at death. Federal estate taxes take the largest bite, although your "taxable" estate must be worth more than $600,000 after significant deductions, such as everything you leave to a spouse, before this tax applies. Estate taxes, both federal and state, must be paid out of your estate before most property can be distributed.

Everything you leave in your will – except what goes to your spouse – is considered part of your taxable estate. In addition, your share of jointly owned property and other property you've left out of the will to avoid probate is part of your taxable estate. (See page 68 for a detailed explanation of what is considered part of your taxable estate.)

If you think that you'll owe estate taxes because your taxable estate is worth more than $600,000, we urge you to consult a professional before drafting your will. You may want your estate plan to include a trust (marital, charitable or other) to help reduce the taxes you'll owe.

State governments typically assess either an estate tax or an *inheritance tax*. An inheritance tax is an excise tax levied against the person inheriting your property.

The tax on any lifetime gifts of more than $10,000 per person per year can have an impact on estate planning. Gifts of more than this amount can increase the amount of estate tax owed on property passed after your death. This tax is called, appropriately enough, a *gift tax*.

Federal Estate Taxes

As mentioned previously, federal estate taxes (also called federal death taxes) don't kick in unless your taxable estate is worth more than $600,000. Because of the $600,000 federal estate tax exemption and the *unlimited marital deduction* (which allows you to give anything or everything to your spouse free of federal estate taxes), most people don't have to pay a federal estate tax.

Federal Estate and Gift Taxes

If your estate is worth more than $600,000, it will be subject to federal taxes of 37 to 55 percent depending on its total value. Here's an example of how this works:

Example
Rachel's taxable estate is worth $2 million. She leaves $1 million to her husband and the rest to her son, Jacob. No federal tax is owed on the money left to her husband because of the unlimited marital deduction – and $600,000 of the $1 million she leaves to Jacob is exempt from tax. Federal estate tax will have to be paid on the remaining $400,000.

Any gifts you make during your lifetime that are over $10,000 each will not be exempt from taxes. Under the Unified Federal Estate and Gift Tax law, gifts and wealth transferred after death are taxed at the same rate; the tax is calculated after you die. This law prevents people from simply giving away their property before they die to escape the federal estate tax.

After you die, any gift you made during your life that amounted to more than $10,000 to any individual during any year lowers your federal estate tax exemption by the excess amount you gave away. You can make gifts of any amount up to and including $10,000 a year to each of as many people as you like without lowering your exemption. Any gifts worth more than the $10,000 per person are subtracted from your $600,000 federal estate tax exemption.

Example

Jeremy gave $50,000 a year to his son and daughter-in-law each year for three years. These were the only large gifts he made. He left his total remaining estate, worth $1 million at his death, to the same son and daughter-in-law. Because Jeremy gave them more than $20,000 a year (that is, more than $10,000 to each of them each year), his estate will not get the full $600,000 federal tax exemption. Instead, he gets an exemption of only $510,000 – the $600,000 reduced by the $90,000 he gave away ($30,000 a year for three years) that exceeded the annual gift allowance. At Jeremy's death, federal taxes are owed on $490,000: the $1 million estate minus the $510,000 federal exemption remaining to him after subtracting the excess gifts.

Lowering the Federal Estate Tax

A 37-percent tax bite is no small matter, and that's the minimum tax that will be paid on any amount over $600,000. But there are estate-planning tools that can lower or eliminate the amount you could owe. While this chapter doesn't cover all of your tax planning needs, it does offer some constructive tips.

Give money to your spouse. Thanks to the unlimited marital deduction, anything passed to your spouse is free of estate tax. If you're a young and healthy couple, naming each other sole beneficiary in your will makes tax sense. If the unexpected occurs and one of you dies, the other will have full access to the estate, something the surviving spouse will probably want and need.

However, if you and your spouse are reasonably wealthy and retired or approaching retirement age, and if your children are grown with families of their own, this may not be the best plan. That's because if you pass everything you own on to your spouse, you may simply be bumping the value of your spouse's estate above the $600,000 federal exemption without benefiting from your own $600,000 exemption.

If you wish to pass assets to your children or someone else you should consider a bypass (or credit-shelter) trust. It can be used to take advantage of your own federal tax credit, lower the value of your spouse's eventual taxable estate, and still give your spouse access to income from your assets (but not the principal) after you die.

Give money to charity. Donations to qualifying charities are not included in your taxable estate. They're deducted from your gross estate, lowering its worth for federal tax considerations.

Give $10,000 ($20,000 if you're a married couple) each year to your heirs. If you know to whom you want to leave your money and can spare it now, you may give tax-free gifts of any amount up to and including $10,000 to each of them every year and thereby reduce the value of your taxable estate.

Create an irrevocable living trust. You can reduce the size of your taxable estate by placing some of your property into an irrevocable living trust. To gain the tax benefits, however, you must give up all control over the property placed in trust, you must have transferred the property into the trust at least three years prior to your death, you cannot get the property back (directly or indirectly) and you do not have the right to change or cancel the trust.

State Taxes

The IRS isn't the only one that wants a piece of your wealth when you die. Every state also imposes a tax on the transfer of a deceased person's property. The three types of state assessments are *inheritance taxes, estate taxes* and *credit-estate taxes*. In most instances, however, these state taxes result in only a minor bite out of your estate.

Credit estate tax. Every state has what is known as a credit estate tax, in effect a federal tax rebate whose net effect is that you pay nothing more than the federal tax. (The amount of tax is the state tax credit the IRS will allow your beneficiaries to deduct from the federal estate tax your estate owes. Like the federal tax, credit-estate tax affects only estates worth more than $600,000.)

Inheritance and estate taxes. Some states impose either an estate tax or an inheritance tax, but usually not both. The significant differences between the two are how the tax is calculated and who must pay it. Estate tax states base the tax rate on the size of the estate. Inheritance tax states base it on the relationship of the beneficiary to the deceased person and the amount each beneficiary inherits.

States that have inheritance taxes usually tax what's left to spouses, children and grandchildren at a lower rate than what's passed to brothers and sisters, for instance, and tax what's left to other beneficiaries (such as cousins or neighbors) at a higher rate. Typically, a spouse's inheritance might be taxed only 1 or 2 percent of the value inherited while an unrelated friend might have to pay as much as 20 percent.

Personal exemptions also apply to these inheritance taxes in many states. As with the tax rates themselves, these exemptions vary from state to state and according to the relationship of the beneficiary to the deceased person. In Iowa, for example, each son and daughter gets the first $50,000 tax-free, while in Montana, they get the entire amount tax-free.

Instead of taxing the inheritance, a few states tax the estate itself. Like the federal estate tax, the state death tax is a percentage of the value of the estate. The more valuable the estate, the higher the percentage. For this tax, the relationship of the beneficiary to the deceased is irrelevant.

Taxes are owed to the state in which the deceased resided; so if you live part of the year in one state and part in another, you might want to establish residency in the state with the most favorable tax laws. Don't bother moving just to save on taxes because it's highly unlikely that the potential savings would be worth the hassle.

State Gift Tax

Delaware, Louisiana, New York, North Carolina, South Carolina, Tennessee and Wisconsin impose a state gift tax using the same rules and rates as their death taxes. Individuals with extremely large estates might consider moving from a state with high taxes to one with more favorable laws if they want to distribute gifts to their heirs during their lifetime.

Lowering Taxes With Trusts

Trusts are perhaps the most important tools for reducing taxes. But don't create a trust prematurely. Remember that you can give away gifts of up to $10,000 a year tax-free to as many individuals as you want; your contributions to a qualifying charitable organization are 100 percent tax-deductible; and if you're married, anything you give to your spouse is a tax-free gift.

Trusts can lower three basic kinds of taxes: income tax, federal estate and gift taxes, and state-imposed estate and gift taxes. Certain "marital trusts" and trusts for children can also be used effectively to reduce taxes, now and when you die.

Figuring Your Taxable Estate

What is your taxable estate for federal estate tax purposes? The basic rule is that your taxable estate includes everything you own, whether it's passed on in your will and subject to probate or not, less deductions, expenses and gifts to charities. You need to determine your taxable estate, because if it's more than $600,000, your beneficiaries will probably have to pay a significant part of it in taxes.

Determine your gross estate. Total the value of all property owned at death. In addition to the obvious (your share of your home, bank accounts, stocks, businesses, furniture and the like), your gross estate also includes:

Trusts. The entire value of any revocable trust you create is included in your gross estate. It's value is what you own and control.

If you create an irrevocable living trust but keep some ownership rights, the value of that right is also added to your estate.

If you're a beneficiary of a trust set up by someone else, the value of your interest in that trust can also be part of your estate.

Normally, if you receive payments from a trust created by someone else, but are not the trustee and the trust goes to someone else when you die, the value of the trust isn't included in your estate.

Intangible property. Property whose market value may be far from obvious, such as patent rights, is also part of your estate.

Life insurance. If you retain the power to change the policy or give that power away less than three years before you die, the value of the policy is included in your estate. If you take out life insurance on someone else and die before that person does, the cash value of the policy is included in your estate.

Subtract deductions from the gross estate. To calculate whether your estate surpasses the federal estate tax threshold of $600,000 and, if it does, how much of it's taxable, subtract from it: all property you leave to your spouse; funeral and last-illness expenses; money you owe and uncollectible money that's owed to you; charitable bequests; probate fees and other fees and expenses for administering the estate.

Once you determine your taxable estate, you can check your tax rate on the federal tax chart in Appendix II. Remember that this tentative tax will be reduced by the tax credit you get for the $600,000 exemption (minus lifetime gifts) as well as other credits, such as those for any state death taxes or estate taxes already paid.

Chapter 10

GETTING HELP

This book provides a step-by-step guide for drafting a simple will. If you need something more than a simple will, don't want to do the work necessary to create a simple will, or simply want your work checked over, this chapter explains your options for getting help.

Low-Cost Options

You have three places to go for low-cost services – legal clinics, legal service plans and independent paralegals. Their availability may depend on where you live. All three specialize in will preparation, but can also provide help with other routine legal matters, such as preparing a living or testamentary trust, durable power of attorney for health care, or living will.

You can get help from a *legal clinic* on most legal matters, including drafting a will, for less than the going rate of local law firms. A Hyatt Legal Services clinic in Washington, D.C., for example, quotes $125 as a figure for drafting a simple will, $50 to $75 for a living will, and $95 for a durable power of attorney. (In Cleveland, Ohio, the quotes were $75, $25 and $70 respectively.) You should consult one of their attorneys in person to discuss prices, what information is needed to prepare your will and how long it will take. They should produce these documents for you within a couple of weeks.

Legal clinics offer services at competitive rates because they limit themselves to routine cases, streamline operations with standard forms, and hire newly trained lawyers and paralegals. If your needs are simple, a legal clinic is definitely worth looking into, but shop around and compare services and prices before buying. As with traditional law firms, the quality of service and costs vary from clinic to clinic. It's up to you to ask questions and get references.

Some legal clinics may review your work after you've drawn up your own will, but may charge a fee that is only slightly less than what it would cost to have them do the will from scratch. Check with legal clinics in your area for prices.

Legal services plans operate something like health maintenance organizations (HMOs). They stress preventive care and serve a defined group of clients. The plans started as an employer-paid benefit for union members, but have since become widely available to other groups and even to individuals. The National Resource Center for Consumers of Legal Services estimates that more than 58.3 million Americans were enrolled in these plans as of August 1990.

Some plans are "prepaid" and require a membership fee up front. Others simply charge enrolled members reduced rates for services. If you belong to a group plan, chances are your employer or union picks up all or most of the membership fee. If you belong to a private or individual plan, you probably pay an annual membership fee of about $100.

Many group plans offer comprehensive services, including preparing wills, trusts, and many other legal documents. Private plans, like those offered by Montgomery Ward or Prepaid Legal Services, Inc., typically offer fewer benefits. Membership in a private plan usually includes unlimited legal advice over the telephone, will preparation, and legal review of documents up to six pages.

If will preparation is the main reason you're joining a plan, make sure the "simple will" offered will take care of your estate-planning needs. Under the Montgomery Ward plan, a simple will "distributes the property generally and does not involve any trusts, complex tax considerations or guardianships for minor children." The plan's simple will is only for people who want to leave their property to one person or divide it equally among a number of people. If you need something more complex, such as creating a children's trust in your will, or if you also want a durable power of attorney for health care or a living will, most plans will refer you to a plan lawyer. These lawyers do the work for a discount, usually 25 to 35 percent less than the going rate charged by local lawyers.

In a growing number of states, *independent paralegals* offer routine legal services to the public. Paralegals don't have a law degree or a license to practice law, but many of them have experience working in law firms and some attended paralegal school. Independent paralegals who sell services to the public typically offer one or two specialized services. Like legal services lawyers, they can offer lower prices and often develop a high level of competence in those services simply by repeatedly preparing the same forms.

Be aware, however, that independent paralegals are not legally permitted to provide legal advice. They may not tell you what type of will is best for you, or advise you on how to complete a will form, or even explain the laws governing wills. Some independent paralegals stay within these guidelines; others find it difficult to restrict themselves to distributing forms and filling in the blanks for you without giving advice on how the forms should be filled out. This is particularly true of those who have prepared numerous estate plans.

The best way to find independent paralegals is by word-of-mouth, by searching newspaper advertisements, or by looking under "paralegals" or "typing services" in the Yellow Pages.

Independent paralegals charge a fraction of what local lawyers charge. If your attorney wants $150 to draft a simple will, chances are you can get an independent paralegal to do it for about $50.

Lawyers

Many people think about hiring a lawyer to draft their will, especially if they have complicated distribution plans for their property, don't have the time, or feel too intimidated to do it on their own. If you decide to hire a lawyer, be sure you're working with someone who is familiar with estate planning. Just because a lawyer has a license to practice law is no assurance that the lawyer regularly prepares wills or is up-to-date on estate-planning laws. If you find an estate-planning lawyer or a general practitioner with estate-planning experience, you can get a will for $150 - $200. A good lawyer will advise you on will clauses that meet your goals, make sure that your will conforms to your state's laws, and advise you on any taxes that may be owed. A lawyer can also suggest an entire estate-planning package, which might include documents like a living will and durable power of attorney for health care, and a number of trust options.

If you don't already have a lawyer and aren't sure how to find one, ask for recommendations from friends, relatives, neighbors or business associates. Other options include getting referrals from your local or state bar associations; checking for names in directories at your local library; or contacting groups such as HALT that have attorney referral services. You will need to interview and compare services, fees and costs. (See HALT's book, *Using a Lawyer: And What To Do If Things Go Wrong*.)

Before discussing fees, the lawyer may want to know a little about your estate, so come prepared to share that information. Use the inventory in Appendix III as a guide.

PART III

SIMPLE
WILL CLAUSES

Chapter 11:

WILL CLAUSES I

Chapters 11, 12 and 13 provide a step-by-step guide for creating a plain-language simple will by assembling the clauses you want.

A will doesn't have to be written in legalese to be valid, but it should contain several specifics: your name (as testator), the person responsible for administering your estate after you die (executor), the person responsible for looking after any minor children (guardian) and a plan for distributing your real estate and personal property (bequests).

The clauses introduced in these chapters also allow you to create a trust to manage a child's inheritance, forgive debts, provide instructions on payment of taxes, discourage will contests, disinherit potential heirs, and even provide for an orphaned pet.

The steps for putting your will together are in Chapter 14, "Writing Your Will." Chapter 14 explains how to assemble your will by using the boxes in the left hand margin of the clauses presented in the next three chapters. *Ignore the boxes when you first read these chapters.*

This book doesn't include clauses for burial instructions or organ donations because, as mentioned in Chapter 3, these instructions are better put in a letter to your executor or other document because your will may not be available immediately upon your death.

The simple will has been grouped into six categories to make it easier for you to follow.

Section I – Introductory Clauses

Title Your Will

Introduce Yourself

Revoke Prior Wills

Section II – Family & Guardian Clauses

Identify Spouse and Children

Establish Survivorship

Name a Guardian

Create a Children's Trust

Section III – Disposition of Property Clauses

Leave Gifts of Personal Property

Leave Gifts of Real Property

Leave Gifts of Money

Leave Your Residuary Estate

Section IV – Special Instruction Clauses

Forgive Debts

Disinherit Potential Heirs

Discourage Will Contests

Provide for Pets

Section V – Executor's Clauses

Name Your Executor

Grant Powers to Your Executor

Pay Your Taxes

Section VI – Signature & Witnesses' Clauses

Sign Your Will

Have Your Will Witnessed (or Attested To)

Self-Prove Your Will

Sections I and II are covered in this chapter, Sections III and IV in Chapter 12, and Sections V and VI in Chapter 13. When drafting your will, you'll be using clauses from each of these sections.

You'll note that clauses are identified as either "mandatory" or "optional." As you might guess, mandatory clauses must be included in your will while optional clauses may or may not apply. Our discussion of each clause will help to clear up any confusion about what you should include in your will.

Sometimes you will be given a choice of clauses, other times you will not.

If you're a Louisiana resident, you can create a will using this book. All you have to do is select clauses from this and the next two chapters and follow the special instructions that apply to your state in Chapter 14.

Section I – Introductory Clauses

This section includes three short clauses. All are mandatory. After titling your will and stating whose will it is, you'll give your first instruction with the clause that revokes all previous wills written (advisable even if you've never written a will before).

 ## Title Your Will

The heading of a will always identifies whose will it is.

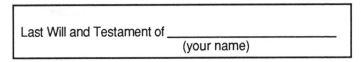

Last Will and Testament of _____
(your name)

 ## Introduce Yourself

This clause identifies you by name and provides information about where you live. When identifying yourself, list your "legal" name first and any other names you commonly use, like a middle name or maiden name. For example, "I, James Francis Jones, also known as, Frankie Jones ..."

When identifying where you live, list your principal place of domicile. If you divide your time evenly between two states – six months in Arizona and six in Alaska – you should check with someone such as a lawyer to see which state you should list as your domicile. This is especially important if you're married and the states where you reside have different marital property ownership laws. It's also important for tax reasons because both states could try to assess death taxes against your estate.

> I, _____,
> (your legal and any commonly used names)
>
> a resident of _____ County
>
> in _____ , being of
> (city and state)
>
> sound mind and memory and not acting under any
>
> duress, fraud or undue influence, declare this to be my
>
> Last Will and Testament.

✔ 1 Revoke Prior Wills

A clause revoking previous wills and *codicils* (amendments to your will) is so standard that even first time will writers include it in their wills. The purpose of this clause is to clear up any confusion over which will is truly your last will.

> I revoke all previous wills and codicils made by me.

Section II – Family & Guardian Clauses

All of the clauses included in this section are optional and have to do with identifying family members, establishing how long a beneficiary must survive you before they can inherit your property, appointing a guardian for minor children, and setting up a trust for minor children.

Identify Spouse and Children

In recent years, it has become customary to include a clause that gives your marital and parental status. It helps to identify the major players in your will, which is particularly important if you plan to disinherit some of those players.

If you're a parent, you should identify, by name, all biological, adopted, and step children from current and previous marriages even if you do not intend to make any of them a beneficiary. By naming all of your children, no child can contest the will by claiming you intentionally or accidentally omitted their names. If you want to disinherit a child or any other person, see the clause on page 100.

The clause option that identifies children commonly includes a provision for future children, either biological or adopted. If you have grandchildren and want to acknowledge them (some states require it) or if you've been married more than once, your will should also include Options Five and Six.

☐ *Option One:*

> I am single and do not have any children.

☐ *Option Two:*

I am single and have _____ children:
   (number of children)

_____,
   (name and date of birth)

_____,
   (name and date of birth)

_____,
   (name and date of birth)

It is my intention that my will include the above named

children and any other children born to or adopted by me

after the date of this will.

☐ *Option Three:*

I am married to _____, herein
   (spouse's name)

referred to as my _____ and together we
   (wife/husband)

have no children.

☐ *Option Four:*

I am married to _____, herein
　　　　　　　(spouse's name)

referred to as my _____ and together we
　　　　　　　　　(wife/husband)

have _____ children.
　　(number of children)

_____,
(name and date of birth)

_____,
(name and date of birth)

_____.
(name and date of birth)

It is my intention that my will include the above named

children and any other children born to or adopted by me

after the date of this will.

☐ *Option Five:*

I have _____ grandchildren.
　　(number of grandchildren)

They are:

_____,
(name and date of birth)

_____.
(name and date of birth)

☐ *Option Six:*

> I was formerly married to _____.
> (name)
>
> Our marriage ended on _____,
> (date)
>
> by _____.
> (death, divorce, annulment)

☐ ☐ **Establish Survivorship**

It's very important, although not mandatory, to include a clause that defines how long a beneficiary must live after your death to inherit your property. This clause sets a 30-day survivorship limit for all beneficiaries. You can adjust the limit if you like, but HALT advises against making the limit longer than 180 days, because that could increase the time and expense of probating your estate. We recommend you include this clause in your will.

> No beneficiary in my will shall be deemed to have
>
> survived me unless living on the 30th day after my death.

☐ ☐ **Name a Guardian**

If you have minor children (under 18 in most states), you should include a clause that names a guardian for them upon your death. You can appoint a guardian to look after their personal and financial needs, or you can split those responsibilities by naming both a personal guardian and a financial guardian. Most parents select one guardian to handle both tasks.

Married couples typically name each other as guardian in their respective wills and a trusted relative, friend or adult child as the alternate or backup guardian. If you're a divorced parent without custody rights, and want to make sure your children are protected in the event your ex-spouse predeceases you, consult a professional for extra help. If you're a divorced parent *with* custody rights, you may designate someone else, besides the other parent, but your choice may not be enforced by the courts.

If you want to appoint a personal care guardian and a second guardian to manage your children's finances, you can use Option Two to appoint separate people for those tasks, with or without a bond requirement.

☐ *Option One:*

If any of my children are still minors at the time of my

death, I nominate _____ to serve
(name)

as guardian over their person and property. If

_____ does not or cannot serve
(name)

for any reason, I nominate _____
(name of alternate guardian)

for the position. No guardian shall be required to furnish

bond.

☐ *Option Two:*

If any of my children are still minors at the time of my

death, I nominate _____
                        (name of personal guardian)

to serve as guardian over their person and

_____ to serve as
        (name of financial guardian)

guardian over their property. If either guardian does not

or cannot serve for any reason, I nominate

_____ to serve as
      (name of alternate personal guardian)

guardian over their person and

_____ to serve as
      (name of alternate financial guardian)

guardian over their property. No guardian shall be

required to furnish bond.

☐ ☐ **Create a Children's Trust**

This clause allows you to create a simple children's trust in your will. It enables you to choose who will manage the trust, how trust funds will be spent on behalf of the child beneficiary and when the trust can be terminated.

A children's trust is usually set up in anticipation of both parents dying before children reach the age of majority (18 years or older in most states). Setting up a children's trust is usually not necessary for married couples who plan to name each other in their respective wills as their children's guardian.

If you're a single parent and you decide you want a children's trust, you should select someone who has your complete confidence as trustee – for example, your child's aunt or uncle. Given the important nature of the job, you should discuss the responsibilities involved ahead of time with the person you plan to designate.

How long the trust lasts is up to you. It can end when the child is any age, though the most common ages are 18, 21, 25, 30 or 35.

If any of my children are _____ years or younger at
                                                  (age)

the time of my death, (and my wife/husband has

predeceased me,) I direct that a trust be created to hold

the property given them under this will. A separate trust

shall be created for each child _____
                                                  (age stated earlier)

years or younger at the time of my death. Each trust shall

end when the beneficiary of that trust turns _____.
                                                  (age funds are to be released)

Clause Continued on Following Page

I nominate _____ to serve as trustee. If
             (name)

_____ does not or cannot serve for any
       (name)

reason, I nominate _____
                        (name of alternate trustee)

for the position. No trustee shall be required to give any

bond or obtain the order or approval of any court in

carrying out any powers or discretion granted in this trust.

The trustee and alternate trustee shall have the full

power and authority allowed by the state of

_____ to manage and distribute
       (name of state)

based on his or her sole discretion the trust's income and

principal on behalf of the beneficiary, including the right

to use income and/or principal for the beneficiary's

education, health (including medical expenses) support

and maintenance. The trust shall terminate when: the

beneficiary turns _____; the beneficiary dies; or the
                   (age funds are to be released)

trust funds are exhausted through distributions allowed

under the provisions of this trust, whichever happens

first. Any trust funds remaining at the termination of the

trust shall pass to the beneficiary, or if no longer living, to

the beneficiary's heirs.

Chapter 12

WILL CLAUSES II

This chapter includes will clauses from Section III, Disposition of Property Clauses, and Section IV, Special Instruction Clauses.

Section III – Disposition of Property Clauses

As mentioned in Chapter 8, there are three ways to leave property to your beneficiaries: a specific bequest, a general bequest or a residuary estate bequest. Although a property distribution clause is not mandatory, it makes little sense to draft a will without one. Many people choose to leave their entire estate to beneficiaries through a residuary estate clause, *or* they make a few specific or general bequests and leave the rest of their estate through the residuary estate clause. This section allows you to choose the best option(s) for you.

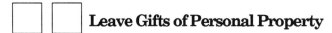 **Leave Gifts of Personal Property**

This clause allows you to give away your personal property. You can give an individual item (such as a painting, a car, an antique clock, the balance on a checking account or a piece of jewelry) or a collection of items (such as, all your tools, clothing, jewelry, or furniture). As mentioned earlier, your description must be exact, for example – my dining room set, grandfather clock, sapphire and diamond ring, 1958 blue Buick. If you want to give cash *and you care where in your estate the money comes from*, state its source – $5,000 from my saving account 123-45-6 at 1st National Bank of Boston. If you don't care, make cash bequests under the "Leave Gifts of Money" clause later in this chapter. You can refresh your memory on some of the ways specific gift clauses can be completed by turning back to Chapter 8 or forward to Appendix IV.

This clause can be selected and duplicated for as many gifts of personal property as you want to make and can also be modified to: delete alternate beneficiaries, identify the relationship of the beneficiary to you, or to add *minor* conditions (for example, leaving money to a relative for their education).

I make the following specific gifts of personal property:

I give _____
(description of property)

to _____
(name of primary beneficiary)

if _____ survives me, or if not, to
(she/he)

_____. If my alternate
(name of alternate beneficiary)

beneficiary does not survive me, I direct that

_____
(description of property)

become a part of my residuary estate and be distributed

accordingly.

Leave Gifts of Real Property

This clause allows you to give away your real estate – that is, any interest you own in a house, condo, co-op or land. You need to be clear about whether the property is entirely yours to give or if only a portion of it is yours to give. Real property that passes to your beneficiary under this clause is subject to any debts on it (mortgages, deed of trusts, liens).

You can select and duplicate this clause for as many gifts of real property as you want to make.

I make the following specific gifts of real property:

I give _____
          (description of property)

to _____
        (name of primary beneficiary)

if _____ survives me, or if not, to
  (she/he)

_____. If my alternate
(name of alternate beneficiary)

beneficiary does not survive me, I direct that

_____
    (description of property)

become a part of my residuary estate and be distributed

accordingly.

If the property identified above is subject to a mortgage,

deed of trust, lien or other encumbrance at the time of

my death, such encumbrances shall pass intact to the

beneficiary receiving that property.

☐ ☐ Leave Gifts of Money

This clause allows you to give away money without stating where it has to come from. Remember, property may have to be sold if you make a general gift of money and there's not enough money in the estate to cover it. Again, the following clause can be duplicated and slightly modified as needed.

I make the following general gifts of money:

I give the sum of _____
                        (amount of cash)

to _____ if _____
        (name of primary beneficiary)   (she/he)

survives me, or if not, to _____.
                              (name of alternate beneficiary)

If my alternate beneficiary does not survive me, I direct

that the sum of _____ become a part of my
                  (amount of cash)

residuary estate and be distributed accordingly.

☐ ☐ Leave Your Residuary Estate

In a residuary estate clause you name the person who will get anything leftover after your specific and general gifts are distributed. As previously mentioned, you might use this clause to give away your entire estate, the bulk of your estate, or any unanticipated last minute inheritances. A residuary clause is often a catch-all clause to include property inherited at the last minute or to distribute specific or general bequests that were not, for whatever reason, given out. Although this clause is not mandatory, it is standard. We strongly recommend you include it in your will.

If you're married and have children, use Option One; if you're single with children, use Option Two. Either option can be modified depending on whether your will creates a children's trust. If it doesn't, delete the second paragraph of the clause you've chosen when drafting your will. For an explanation of per stirpes, see Chapter 8.

If you want to leave your residuary estate to one person, use Option Three. If you want to leave it to two or more people in equal shares, use Option Four.

☐ *Option One:*

I give the residue of my estate, whether real or personal

and wherever situated, to my (wife/husband)

_____ if _____

(name of spouse)   (she/he)

survives me. If my (wife/husband) does not survive me,

then I give the residue in equal shares, one to each of my

children if they survive me. If any of my children should

not survive me, I give their share to their children or

issue, if they have any, per stirpes.

Notwithstanding the foregoing, if my spouse does not

survive me and any child of mine has not

reached the age of _____ at the time of my death, all
(same age stated in your children's trust clause, page 90)

such property to be distributed to such child shall be

distributed to the trustee named herein, to be held,

administered and distributed as instructed under the

terms of the children's trust provision.

☐ *Option Two:*

I give the residue of my estate, whether real or personal

and wherever situated, in equal shares, one to each of

my children who survive me. If any of my children should

not survive me, I give their share to their children or

issue, if they have any, per stirpes.

Notwithstanding the foregoing, if any child of mine has

not reached the age of _____ at the time of my death, all
(same age stated in your children's trust clause, page 90)

such property to be distributed to such child shall be

distributed to the trustee named herein, to be held,

administered and distributed as instructed under the

terms of the children's trust provision.

☐ *Option Three:*

I give the residue of my estate, whether real or personal

and wherever situated, to _____
                                   (name of primary beneficiary)

if _____ survives me. If_____ does not survive
        (she/he)   (she/he)

me, than I give the residue of my estate to

_____.
(name of alternate beneficiary)

If my alternate beneficiary fails to survive me, than I give

the residue of my estate to

_____.
(name of alternate successor /charity)

☐ *Option Four:*

I give the residue of my estate in equal shares, whether

real or personal and wherever situated, to

_____ if _____
(names of primary beneficiaries)   (they)

survive me. If any of my named beneficiaries do not

survive me, than (his/her) share shall go to my surviving

beneficiary(s) in equal shares. If all of my beneficiaries fail

to survive me, than I give the residue of my estate to

_____.
(name of alternate successor /charity)

Section IV – Special Instruction Clauses

This section includes four optional clauses. They allow you to forgive debts, disinherit individuals, discourage will contests and provide for orphaned pets.

☐ ☐ **Forgive Debts**

You can include a clause in your will that forgives debts owed to you by friends or relatives. (If you're married and a debt is owed equally to you and your spouse, you cannot forgive the debt without your spouse's permission.) To be sure your executor knows exactly who you're letting off the hook, be sure to include the name and address of the person who owes you money (*debtor*). (Note: If someone still owes you money at the time of your death and you haven't forgiven the debt, it's your executor's legal duty to try and collect what's owed and distribute it as a part of your estate.)

I forgive the following debts owed to me at the time of my

death by the following persons:

_____
(name of debtor, address, amount owed)

_____
(name of debtor, address, amount owed)

_____
(name of debtor, address, amount owed)

☐ ☐ **Disinherit Potential Heirs**

You can disinherit anyone you want, but your spouse may be entitled to a certain portion of your estate, in addition to any property he or she owns with you jointly. (See Chapter 7 and Appendix I.) Remember, if you're a Louisiana resident, you're not allowed to disinherit children under age 25.

There are several ways to disinherit potential heirs. You can do it by making a general statement, or you can specifically name the individual(s) you want disinherited. It's much safer to name the individual.

☐ *Option One:*

> I disinherit any person not specifically named in my Last
>
> Will and Testament.

☐ *Option Two:*

> I specifically disinherit _____
>   (name)
>
> of _____
>   (full address)
>
> and anyone else not named in my Last Will and
>
> Testament.

☐ ☐ **Discourage Will Contests**

If you're concerned about possible fights among your beneficiaries over how your estate is to be distributed, you may want to include the following clause. It may help reduce the chance of will contests from named beneficiaries, because it disinherits any beneficiary who contests the will. (Of course, if they win the will contest in court this clause is superseded.) There is no way to protect your estate from the truly disgruntled – people not

named in your will or those who were named but
were disinherited – but keep in mind less than 4
percent of all wills are contested.

> If any of my beneficiaries choose to contest or attack my
>
> will, or any of its provisions, his or her share under this will
>
> shall be deemed revoked and distributed as if the
>
> contesting beneficiary had predeceased me without any
>
> children.

Provide For Pets

This clause provides instructions on what
should be done with an orphaned pet(s). It allows
an executor to spend whatever money it takes to
place the pet in a new loving home (for example,
advertising the pet's availability, paying for a
medical checkup or shots, and transportation
costs to the new home). It's assumed the new
owner will pick up any costs associated with the
pet's care, but you can also leave the new owner
money for that expressed purpose.

> I direct my executor to find a caring home for
>
> _____, my pet _____. Any
> (name of pet)   (type of animal)
>
> reasonable expense associated with finding a new home
>
> for my pet are to be paid out of my residuary estate.

Chapter 13

WILL CLAUSES III

This chapter contains will clauses from Section V, Executor's Clauses, and Section VI, Signature and Witnesses' Clauses.

Section V – Executor's Clauses

This section, which allows you to name your executor and give him or her the power to settle your estate, includes three mandatory clauses. All must be included in your will.

 **Name Your Executor**

You will use this clause to choose who will be responsible for settling your estate after you die. You should pick someone who can handle the responsibility, or who can hire and manage appropriate help. An executor's tasks include: inventorying property, filing tax forms, paying debts, making court appearances and distributing property. He or she may also have to run your business operations or sell stock depending on the estate you leave. (See Chapter 6 for a full discussion on executors.)

Option One allows you to select one executor, while Option Two provides for co-executors. Both options provide for backup or alternate executors.

☐ *Option One:*

I nominate _____
                    (name of executor)

to serve as the executor of my estate. If she/he does

not or cannot serve for any reason, I nominate

_____ for the position.
        (name of alternate executor)

Any appointed executor shall not be required to post a

bond.

☐ *Option Two:*

I nominate _____ and
                    (name of executor)

_____ to serve as co-executors
        (name of executor)

of my estate with _____ having
                            (name of executor)

the right to make final decisions if disagreements arise. If

one of the named executors cannot or does not serve

for any reason, the remaining executor can serve alone.

If both executors are unable to serve, I nominate

_____ for the position.
        (name of alternate executor)

Any appointed executor shall not be required to post a

bond.

Grant Powers to Your Executor

Executors are typically granted broad administrative powers so they don't have to petition the probate court every time they need to make a quick decision or fulfill a routine obligation. The following clause lists powers typically given to an executor.

My executor shall have the authority to perform any act

he or she thinks necessary and in the best interest of my

estate and descendants, with no limitations, and

consistent with the laws of _____.

                                    (name of your state)

In addition, my executor is authorized to:

a. retain, until distribution and without liability for loss or

depreciation resulting from such retention, any of my

assets which shall come into his or her possession as a

result of administering my estate.

b. mortgage, lease, pledge, exchange, partition, or sell

any of my assets without prior court order, whether real or

personal, at public or private sale and to invest or reinvest

the proceeds from any sale in the best interest of my

estate.

Clause Continued on Following Page

c. pass any real or personal property which is encumbered by a mortgage, deed of trust, lease or any other loan obligation that requires the payment of money, to the recipient of that particular property.

d. exercise or sell any or all conversion, subscription, option, voting and other rights of whatsoever nature pertaining to any such property, and in their discretion to vote, in person or by proxy, with respect to any matters regarding stocks, securities or other assets constituting part of my estate.

e. retain and continue to operate any business, incorporated or otherwise, which is a part of my estate, including the right to effectuate any plan of corporate or business reorganization, consolidation, merger or similar plan.

f. prosecute, compromise, settle or submit to arbitration any claim in favor or against my estate.

Clause Continued on Following Page

g. appoint and pay a reasonable compensation to any

agent, representative or attorney hired to handle any

matter concerning my estate.

h. settle my estate without intervention of any court,

except to the extent required by law.

 Pay Your Taxes

You have a legal obligation to pay your taxes. Although your will is not invalid without this clause, you might as well have some say about how this obligation is met.

Most people instruct their executor to pay taxes out of their residuary estate, because it's easier to figure out how much the residuary beneficiary(s) will receive once tax computations have been made. You'll owe taxes on the value of your entire estate, not just property that you bequest in your will. So, for example, the value of a jointly owned home or bank account or any property left in a revocable living trust has to be included to figure any taxes you may owe. However, as discussed in Chapter 9, many people owe little or no taxes on their estate after they die.

I direct that my executor pay all estate, inheritance and

other taxes assessed against my estate, including assets

passing under or outside of my will, out of my residuary

estate.

Section VI – Signature &Witnesses' Clauses

To create a valid will, your signature and the signatures of at least three disinterested witnesses must be included in your will. Although it's not required and doesn't effect a will's validity, we also urge you to draft, sign and attach a self-proving affidavit to your will. It can simplify the process of proving that the will is indeed yours after you die.

✔ ☐   **Sign Your Will**

This critical clause provides the space you need to sign and date your will. In the next chapter, we explain exactly what you need to do *before* taking this big step.

IN WITNESS WHEREOF I have signed this Will on this

_____ day of _____ ,

19_____ in _____ .
                    (city/state)

                              _____
                              (your signature)

                              _____
                              (your name typed)

✔ ☐   **Have Your Will Witnessed**
                    (or Attested To)

The number of people required to witness you signing your will varies in each state. Since no state requires more than three witnesses, we suggest you use three (although having more than the necessary number does not invalidate your will).

The witnesses' (or attestation) clause is the written and signed statement of your witnesses. To have a valid will, you must have these witnesses' signatures to prove that your will has been properly executed. The next chapter explains what your witnesses need to do before signing under this clause.

The foregoing instrument, consisting of _____
(number)

pages, including this witness page, was declared, signed

and published by _____ as his/her
(your name)

Last Will and Testament in the presence of us, who were

all present at the same time, and who, in his/her

presence and at his/her request, have signed our names

as witnesses. We declare that to the best of our

knowledge, _____ appeared to be of
(your name)

legal age, of sound mind and memory and under no

constraint or undue influence at the time he/she

executed the foregoing instrument. We declare this to

be true under penalty of perjury.

_____
(signature and address of witness)

_____
(signature and address of witness)

_____
(signature and address of witness)

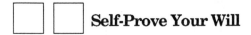

Self-Prove Your Will

(Self-Proving Affidavit)

To simplify the will admission process, most states have enacted legislation that allows you to make your will self-proving. A self-proved will eliminates the need for the witnesses to later testify (in court or otherwise) to theirs' and your signatures, because they have already done so on a signed and notarized affidavit attached to your will. The affidavit makes challenges to your will more difficult, but does not provide an absolute safeguard against them.

You should seriously consider executing a self-proving affidavit with your witnesses, especially if there is any chance they may be difficult to locate after you die.

Appendix I identifies states where the following self-proving affidavit is best used and states where it's advisable to use a locally drafted affidavit. If you live in a state that requires a locally produced affidavit, you may find sample self-proving affidavit forms at the registrar of wills at the probate court, from a local notary, legal stationery store or a local attorney.

Self-Proving Affidavit

STATE OF _____

COUNTY OF _____

We, _____,

_____,

_____ and

_____,

the testator and witnesses respectively, whose names

are signed to the attached or foregoing instrument,

being first duly sworn, do declare to the undersigned

officer that the testator declared, signed and executed

the foregoing instrument as his/her Last Will and

Testament; signed willingly (or willingly directed another

to sign for him/her); executed the foregoing instrument

as his/her free and voluntary act for the purposes therein

expressed. We also declare that each of the witnesses,

in the presence of the testator and at his/her request and

in the presence of each other, signed the foregoing

instrument as a witness and that to the best of his/her

knowledge the testator was at the time of legal age, of

sound mind and memory and under no constraint or

undue influence.

Clause Continued on Following Page

_____
(signature of testator)

_____
(signature and address of witness)

_____
(signature and address of witness)

_____
(signature and address of witness)

Subscribed and sworn to before me by

_____,

the testator, and by _____,

_____ and _____,

the witnesses, on this the _____ day of _____,

19 _____.

                        _____

(Seal)   Notary Public

                  My Commission Expires:

PART IV

DRAFTING YOUR WILL

Chapter 14

WRITING YOUR WILL

This chapter teaches you how to assemble the will clauses presented in Chapters 11 through 13. If you take your time and carefully follow the 10 simple steps, you'll soon realize how easy it is to assemble your will. (To execute a legally valid will in Louisiana, you must follow a slightly different procedure. The most important difference is that your will *must* be notarized.)

Will clauses do not have to be presented in any particular order, but to make your will as airtight as possible, we've set up a system for identifying and numbering your will clauses that protects against any crucial omissions. Note that the will clauses in Chapter 11 through 13 have been identified as either "mandatory" or "optional." Mandatory clauses must be included in a will otherwise the will could be considered invalid and thrown out of court. You may or may not use the optional clauses though we let you know when an optional clause is strongly recommended.

Your final, typed will should be on 8-1/2" x 11" white typing paper. It can be single or double-spaced, but it should allow for one-inch margins all around and it should be typed in upper- and lower-case fashion.

Here's two things you need to do before you get started:

- To avoid flipping back and forth between the pages in this book, copy Chapters 11-13 and work off the photocopied sheets. It'll be easier to fill in the clauses on the photocopied sheets and, if you need to start again, you can get a clean copy of the page or chapter you're working on.

• Read about your state's laws in Appendix I
  and complete the inventory form found in
  Appendix III *before* you begin drafting
  your will.

It may take a few hours, few days or even a few
weeks to finalize your will depending on how
quickly you work, and if you have easy access to
information about your assets. You shouldn't
start drafting until you know you have some
uninterrupted time to work. You may find logical
starting and stopping places; for instance, by
completing steps 1 through 4 one day; 5 through 7
the next, and so on.

With a photocopy of Chapter 11 through 13 and
the completed property inventory form in hand,
you're ready to draft your will by following the 10
steps in this chapter.

Step 1: Pick Relevant Clauses

The first step is to pick the clauses you want to
include in your will. Part of this job – picking
clauses – has already been done for you. You'll
notice when you look at Chapter 11 through 13 that
each clause title is accompanied by two boxes in
the left margin.

The clauses that have already been checked off
for you are the "mandatory" clauses. All
mandatory clauses must appear in your will. The
rest of the clauses are considered "optional." Read
all the optional clauses and place a check mark in
the first of the two boxes of any optional clause you
want to include in your will.

For example, there are six options to choose
from for "Identify Spouse and Children." If you
decide you want to include a clause that identifies
your marital status in your will, place a check
mark in the first box by the clause title and then
another check mark in one of the smaller boxes
next to the option(s) you want. By putting a check
mark in the box next to the title, you'll be able to go

back to the beginning to assemble the clauses in proper order.

Although most of the clauses presented are "optional," pick all the option clauses that apply to your situation. To decide whether or not to include a clause, ask yourself questions like: "Are there debts I want to forgive?" "Do I want to establish a children's trust?" "Is there someone I want to disinherit?"

Step 2: Assemble Clauses in Order

After picking your clauses, assemble them in order. As mentioned, there's no legally required sequence, but there is a standard order HALT recommends you use.

To order the clauses, go back to the clause titles now checked and number them sequentially. Note that number "1" already appears in the second box of the revocation clause. That is where you should start numbering. Put a number "2" in the box beside the next checked-off clause title, a "3" in the following one, and so on.

For example, if you have checked the box by the "Identify Spouse and Children" clause, you should have a number "2" in the second box by that title. Continue your numbering for the second boxes.

When you have completed the numbering, the boxes in the left margin will either be checked off by us (because they're mandatory) or checked off and numbered by you (because you want some optional clauses included as well).

Step 3: Fill in Clauses

After you've checked off and numbered your clauses, fill in the blanks in those clauses. Use a pencil so that you can fix mistakes more easily. In addition to filling in the clauses, you need to cross out any instructional material written right below the spaces to be filled in.

For example, you would complete the following clause:

> I am married to ___*Sally Spouse*___, herein referred to as ~~(spouse's name)~~
>
> my _____*wife*_____ and together we have no children.
> ~~(wife/husband)~~

Step 4: Assemble Clauses & Proofread Your Will

When you've completed the clauses, you can create the first draft of your will. Your draft can be handwritten, typewritten or prepared on a computer. If you have access to a computer, by all means use it. It allows you to make changes and corrections more quickly.

Your draft should include all mandatory clauses and any optional clauses *you* checked off. Assemble the clauses in the order they appear. Start each clause with the number found in its second box. For example, your draft should start to look like this (the title and clause that introduces you – which have a "0" in their second boxes – do not need numbers).

Last Will and Testament of Joan McGinty

I, Joan McGinty, a resident of Middlesex County in Belmont, Massachusetts, being of sound mind and memory and not acting under any duress, fraud or undue influence, declare this to be my Last Will and Testament.

1. I revoke all previous wills and codicils made by me.

2. I am single and do not have any children.

Continue transcribing each clause that is checked with its number until you reach the signature clause. Then transcribe the signature and witnessing clauses leaving appropriate blank spaces for your signature and your witnesses' signatures.

Read over your draft and make sure it includes all the clauses you've checked off from the photocopied sheets. Make sure you've included any clauses that may have been duplicated, such as a specific gift clause. Correct any errors or omissions. *Do not sign* your will at this point as it is only a first draft.

Step 5: Type Your Will

When you're satisfied you have all the clauses you want and your draft is error-free, prepare your final copy. You can type it yourself or hire a typist. Remember, your final will should be on 8-1/2" x 11" white sheets of paper. Each page of your will should be numbered as follows: "Page One of Three," "Page Two of Three," and "Page Three of Three," etc.

Step 6: Proofread For Mistakes

Proofread the final copy of your will for any mistakes. Try to have someone else proofread it as well.

Step 7: Correct Any Mistakes & Make Photocopies

Regardless of how minor an error may be, do not attempt to make corrections in pen, pencil, by using liquid correction fluid or any other "surface" correction. If you find a mistake, you need to retype the page it appears on or, if necessary, retype the entire will. Your final will must be typewritten from start to finish without mistake. If it takes a few attempts, that's what it will take to have a valid will. Once you have a completely error-free original of your will, you should make two photocopies and mark each one "COPY." These copies won't include your signature because you haven't signed your will yet.

The original will, if more than one page, should be stapled together in the top left corner. Do this for each of the two photocopies as well. Do not remove the staple from the original version for any reason. If you do, it might raise suspicions that your will was tampered with and could ultimately invalidate your will.

It's important to make copies of your will, because if something should happen to your original at least there is a copy to show the probate judge. While a photocopy of your will cannot usually be submitted for probate – it can influence the judge to carry out your intentions instead of strictly following your state's intestacy laws.

Step 8: Gather Your Witnesses

Before signing your will, you need to bring together the people who will witness your will. Three witnesses will satisfy the statutory requirements in every state. Your witnesses should not be people named in your will. They might be co-workers, friends or neighbors. Whomever you select, pick witnesses who are 18 years or older and who could testify they signed your will as a witness, if ever called upon to do so. *Do not pick* a beneficiary or guardian as witness.

The people you choose do not have to know you nor do they have to read your will. All they have to do is swear (by signing the witnesses' clause) that they witnessed you signing the will. In Louisiana, witnesses must read the will, (see page 124).

Step 9: Sign, Witness & Self-Prove Your Will

When you've called all your witnesses together, you must tell them: "This is my Last Will and Testament. I am about to sign and date it and am asking each of you to be a witness to my signature."

At this point, you can sign and date your will. If it's more than a page, you should initial and date each page in the bottom right hand corner. This is not legally required, but it helps prove that there were no page substitutions. Then pass your will to each of your witnesses. Ask each to read the attestation clause and then to sign in the space provided below that clause. All your witnesses must sign *in your presence* and *in the presence of each other in the same room at the same time.* They should also print, under or to the side of their signature, their name and address.

Congratulations! You now have drafted and executed a legally valid will.

If you plan to attach a self-proving affidavit to your will, you and your witnesses need to appear all together before a notary. You can sign your will and attach a signed self-proving affidavit at the same time, if you have a notary present. If that's not convenient, you and your witnesses can collectively meet with a notary at a later time, after the will has been signed and witnessed. The notary will ask you and each witness to print your names in the spaces provided in the affidavit. The notary will read the affidavit out loud and ask you and your witnesses to swear to the truth of the statements made in it. You and each witness then sign the affidavit and it is notarized.

You should staple the notarized affidavit to the end of your will.

Step 10: Store Your Will

The original and photocopies of your will should be stored in separate places. You should file your original will in a safe place such as:

- With the probate registrar at your county courthouse, if they allow the will to be filed before death (usually for free or a small fee).
- With a family member or close friend.
- Where you keep other important papers – for instance, in a fire-proof file drawer.

It's unwise to keep your original will in a safe-deposit box because your state's laws may require that the box be sealed for a period of time after your death or that special procedures be used in opening it, such as asking witnesses to be present, which could delay the process.

You should keep copies of your will where it can be found easily after your death. Give a copy of your will to your executor and another to a trusted friend or relative. Inform family members and anyone else who is appropriate of its location. It's also a good idea to keep your Letter of Instruction with your will.

LOUISIANA RESIDENTS

If your witnesses live outside of the area where your will is being executed in, or if, for whatever reason, you cannot follow the instructions as described below, do not attempt to draft your will using this book. Seek professional help, which in Louisiana can include contacting a notary. Louisiana notaries not only can notarize documents, but also perform many of the same legal tasks that lawyers do, such as drafting wills, forming corporations, and giving legal advice.

How To Execute a Louisiana Will

To prepare your will in Louisiana you will identify and number will clauses from Chapters 11 through 13 the same way as everyone else. However, when you come to the will clause identified on page 108 as "Sign Your Will," replace it with the following:

IN WITNESS THEREOF, I have signed this LAST WILL

AND TESTAMENT, in the presence of the witnesses

and notary hereinafter named and undersigned.

_____
(your name)

Also replace the next clause, titled "Have Your Will Witnessed (or Attested To)," with the following language:

State of Louisiana, Parish of _____

Signed on each of the foregoing _____ pages,
                                   (number)

and declared by _____, the testator (testatrix)
                 (your name)

above named, in our presence, to be his (her) last will

and testament, and in the presence of the testator

(testatrix) and of each other, we have hereunto

subscribed our names as witnesses on this _____ day

of _____, 19_____, at _____,
                                     (city/parish/state)

within and for which the undersigned Notary Public is

duly commissioned, qualified and sworn.

_____
(your name)

Clause Continued on Following Page

```
┌─────────────────────────────────────────────────┐
│                                                   │
│  WITNESSES:                                       │
│                                                   │
│  _____│
│     (signature and address of witness)            │
│                                                   │
│  _____│
│     (signature and address of witness)            │
│                                                   │
│  _____│
│     (signature and address of witness)            │
│                                                   │
│                                                   │
│                  _____     │
│                  Notary Public                    │
│                                                   │
│                  State of Louisiana               │
│                                                   │
│                  Parish of:                       │
│                                                   │
│                  My Commission Expires:           │
│                                                   │
└─────────────────────────────────────────────────┘
```

Now, follow the same steps for creating a draft of your will as outlined in this chapter up to and including Step 8. Make sure the last page of your will contains spaces for the date, your signature, your witnesses' signatures and the notary's signature.

When you have created an error-free – and unsigned – typewritten draft of your will, make a copy for each of your witnesses and one for the notary. Then you and your witnesses must go to a notary (or make plans to have a notary come to you).

When you are all gathered together in a closed-off room, read your will out loud from top to bottom. When you're done, make a statement similar to the following to your witnesses: "This is my Last Will and Testament. I am about to sign and date it and am asking each of you to be a witness to my signature."

At this point, you can sign and date your will. If your will is more than one page, place your full signature on the bottom of each page. After you're done, pass your will to each of your witnesses for their signatures.

In Louisiana, you and your witnesses are required to sign in the presence of each other and in the presence of the notary to create a valid will. The notary will then sign and notarize your document. You don't need to execute a separate self-proving affidavit in Louisiana.

Chapter 15:

A SIMPLE WILL

This chapter contains a model simple will for a married father with three adult children. He appoints his wife, Irene, executor of his estate. He makes three specific gifts to long-time friends, and gives the rest of his property to his wife. If Irene predeceases him, his property will be distributed per stirpes to his children – meaning each will get one-third of his estate, or, if any child has died, his or her children will share equally that one-third.

**Last Will and Testament of
Christopher John Koller**

I, Christopher John Koller, a resident of Hennepin County in Minneapolis, Minnesota, being of sound mind and memory and acting freely and voluntarily, declare this to be my Last Will and Testament.

1. I revoke all previous wills and codicils made by me.

2. I am married to Irene Janice Koller, herein referred to as my wife and together we have four children: Alexander James Koller born July 8, 1950, Chantal Marie Legeux born November 13, 1954, Karen M. Emter born October 3, 1956 and Mark Daniel Koller born June 19, 1958. It is my intention that my will shall include the above named children and any other children born to or adopted by me after the date of this will.

3. No beneficiary in my will shall be deemed to have survived me unless living on the 30th day after my death.

Continued on Following Page

4. I make the following specific gifts of personal property:

I give the rights to my U.S. Patent #4050439 to my long-time friend Michael R. Chellis if he survives me, or if not, to my good friend Rebecca Noel. If my alternate beneficiary does not survive me, I direct that this patent right become a part of my residuary estate and be distributed accordingly.

I give my 1934 and 1951 Chevrolets to my old friend Dennis J. Boyle if he survives me, or if not, I direct that my 1934 and 1951 Chevrolets become a part of my residuary estate and be distributed accordingly.

I give my cigar label collection to my good friend Salvatore Ales if he survives me, or if not, I direct that my cigar label collection become a part of my residuary estate and be distributed accordingly.

5. I give the residue of my estate, whether real or personal and wherever situated, to my wife Irene if she survives me. If my wife does not survive me, than I give the residue in equal shares, one to each of my children who survive me. If any of my children should not survive me, I give their share to their children or issue, if they have any, per stirpes.

6. I direct my executor to find a caring home for Baby Bald, my pet cockatoo. Any reasonable expense associated with finding a new home for my pet are to be paid out of my residuary estate.

7. I nominate my son, Alexander, to serve as the executor of my estate. If he does not or cannot serve for any reason, I nominate my son Mark for the position. Any appointed executor shall not be required to post a bond.

Clause Continued on Following Page

8. My executor shall have the authority to perform any act he thinks necessary and in the best interest of my estate and descendants, with no limitations and consistent with the laws of Minnesota. In addition, my executor is authorized to:

a. retain, until distribution and without liability for loss or depreciation resulting from such retention, any of my assets which shall come into his or her possession as a result of administering my estate.

b. mortgage, lease, pledge, exchange, partition, or sell any of my assets without prior court order, whether real or personal, at public or private sale and to invest or reinvest the proceeds from any sale in the best interest of my estate.

c. pass any real or personal property which is encumbered by a mortgage, deed of trust, lease or any other loan obligation which requires the payment of money, to the recipient of that particular property.

d. exercise or sell any or all conversion, subscription, option, voting and other rights of whatsoever nature pertaining to any such property, and in their discretion to vote, in person or by proxy, with respect to any matters regarding stocks, securities or other assets constituting part of my estate.

e. retain and continue to operate any business, incorporated or otherwise, which is a part of my estate, including the right to effectuate any plan of corporate or business reorganization, consolidation, merger or similar plan.

f. prosecute, compromise, settle or submit to arbitration any claim in favor or against my estate.

g. appoint and pay a reasonable compensation to any agent, representative or attorney hired to handle any matter concerning my estate.

h. settle my estate without intervention of any court, except to the extent required by law.

9. I direct that my executor pay all estate, inheritance and other taxes assessed against my estate, including assets passing under or outside of my will, out of my residuary estate.

Continued on Following Page

IN WITNESS WHEREOF I have signed this Will on this 15th day of August, 1991 in Minneapolis, Minnesota.

Christopher John Koller

(Christopher John Koller)

The foregoing instrument, consisting of three pages, including this witness page, was declared, signed and published by Christopher John Koller as his Last Will and Testament in the presence of us, who were all present at the same time, and who, in his presence and at his request, have signed our names as witnesses. We declare that to the best of our knowledge, Christopher John Koller appeared to be of legal age, of sound mind and memory and under no constraint or undue influence at the time he executed the foregoing instrument. We declare this to be true under penalty of perjury.

Elizabeth Jane Barrow, 59 Cross Street, Minneapolis, MN

Nicholas Joseph Wiley, 87 Douglas Road, Minneapolis, MN

James Ralph Winters, 124 Maple Street, Minneapolis, MN

UPDATING WILLS

Read your will every few years to make sure that it is current and still accomplishes what you want. You'll need to update your will anytime there is a major change in your life or in your state's estate laws. In particular, check your will to see if it needs updating when:

- You get married or remarried.
- You become widowed or divorced.
- Your feelings about a primary beneficiary change because for instance, they win the lottery and no longer need your money.
- Estate tax laws change drastically.
- You move to a new state or buy real estate out of state.
- You need to change beneficiaries (often happens when a child is born, adopted or dies).
- You wish to make different bequests.
- The executor or guardian you named in the will can no longer serve.

You can change your will at anytime and for any reason by using a *codicil*, which is attached to your will, or revoking your old will and drafting a new one. Don't make changes to your will by writing on the will or by crossing out sentences or entire clauses. That could invalidate the whole will. If you draft an amendment or write a new will, you'll need to draft a new self-proving affidavit.

Writing a New Will

It makes sense to prepare a new will if there are major changes in your life that effect your estate plan (for example, you get married, or divorced or a child becomes disabled), or if you have several minor changes you need to make at once.

Use discretion when drafting codicils. If a codicil makes too dramatic a change, it could confuse your executor, beneficiaries and the court. For example, you should not leave a substantial portion of your estate to your son and then use a codicil to disinherit that son.

Revoking Your Will. Anytime you write a new will, you should include a clause revoking any previously written will. The mere act of writing a new will may revoke any previous will, but to be sure everyone is clear, you should always include a revocation clause.

You may revoke your will by destroying it – putting it in a shredder, burning it or defacing each page in some way will revoke your will. In some states, your will is automatically revoked if you get married or divorced. (See Appendix I for a list of these states.) It's a good idea to physically destroy a will any time you wish to revoke it, even if you have drafted a new one with a revocation clause.

Anyone who has the original copy of your will should give it back so you can destroy it. If they don't, don't worry. Your new will with a revocation clause is all you really need. You don't need anyone's permission to draft a new will.

Updating an Existing Will

Simple changes, like changing the name of an executor or guardian or adding an additional specific bequest, can easily be handled by amending your will with a codicil.

A codicil is a separate and new document that updates your will. Because it's legally part of your will, it must be executed just like a will. It must be typed, signed and witnessed.

Here's a sample codicil:

First Codicil to the Last Will and Testament of Thomas Bradford Bishop

I, Thomas Bradford Bishop, a resident of Putnam County in Carmel, New York, being of sound mind and memory and not acting under any duress, fraud or undue influence, declare this to be the First Codicil to my Last Will and Testament, executed October 3, 1990.

Clause 5 of my Last Will and Testament is hereby revoked, in its entirety and the following is substituted for it:

> I nominate my wife, Elizabeth W.F. Bishop to serve as the executor of my estate. If she does not or cannot serve for any reason, I nominate my good friend Andrew Joseph Mooney, for the position. Any appointed executor shall not be required to post bond.

To Clause 8 of my Last Will and Testament, I add:

> I give $5,000 to my neighbor Pamela Brown if she survives me, or if not, to her son Patrick Brown. If my alternate beneficiary does not survive me, I direct that the $5,000 become a part of my residuary estate and be distributed accordingly.

Clause 10 of my Last Will and Testament is hereby revoked in its entirety.

Other than the changes stated herein, I confirm and republish my Last Will and Testament as referred to above on this the 25th day of November, 1991.

Thomas Bradford Bishop
(Thomas Bradford Bishop)

This codicil was signed, published and declared by Thomas Bradford Bishop on November 25, 1991 in the presence of all of us. At his request and in his presence and in the presence of each other, we now sign as witnesses and declare that to the best of our knowledge he appeared to be of legal age, of sound mind and memory and under no constraint or undue influence at the time he executed this codicil. We declare this to be true under penalty of perjury.

Janet E. Fishstein, 3535 Monroe Lane, New York, NY

David Whipple, 98 Liverpool Street, New York, NY

Steven Hinkamp, 9 Davis Street, New York, NY

Drafting a codicil is just like drafting a really short will; the steps are the same. As when drafting your will using this book, the boxes in the left margin alert you to "mandatory" and "optional" codicil clauses. Mandatory clauses are checked off and must appear in your codicil. Clauses that are not checked are optional and may be used for as many changes as you need.

To Prepare Your Codicil

Step 1. Place a check mark in the boxes beside the optional clauses you want to use.

Step 2. Draft your codicil by typing or writing all checked-off clauses on paper or into your computer.

Step 3. Print a typed draft on white 8-1/2" x 11" sheets of paper. Proofread it and, if necessary, correct it. As with a will, don't make corrections in pen, with liquid correction fluid or any other topical method. If the codicil is more than a page, number the pages as you did for your will. Remember, your final version must be completely error free.

Step 4. When you have an error-free draft, gather your witnesses and make the following statement to them: "This is the first codicil to my Last Will and Testament. I am about to sign and date it and am asking each of you to be a witness to my signature."

Step 5. Sign the codicil, have your witnesses read the attestation clause, and then ask each of them to sign in front of you and each other. If you plan to execute a self-proving affidavit for your codicil (see page 139), that too needs to be drafted, typed on white 8-1/2" x 11" typing paper, proofread, corrected and signed by you and your witnesses in front of a notary.

Codicil Clauses

☑ *Start With a Title and Introduction:*

First Codicil to Last Will and Testament of

_____
     (your name)

I, _____, a resident
     (your name)

of _____, County in _____,
    (county)   (city, state)

being of sound mind and memory and not acting under

any duress, fraud or undue influence, declare this to be

the First Codicil to my Last Will and Testament executed

_____.
   (date original will was executed)

☐ *If You Want to Substantially Change a Clause, Use:*

Clause _____ of my Last Will and Testament is

hereby revoked in its entirety, and the following is

substituted for it:

(First identify the clause you're replacing by putting its

number in the space provided. Then in this space, write

the clause as you now want it stated. If the clause is

substantially the same, for example, you're just changing

the names of a primary and alternate executor, you

should use language from the clause in your original will.)

☐ *If You Want To Add Information to An Existing Clause, Use:*

To Clause _____ of my Last Will and Testament I add:

(Again, identify the clause you're making additions to by

putting its number in the space provided. In this space,

include the language you want added to the clause

identified.)

☐ *If You Want To Revoke a Clause in Its Entirety and Not Replace It, Use:*

Clause _____ of my Last Will and Testament is

hereby revoked in its entirety.

✔ *Then Include the Following Closing Language:*

Other than the changes stated herein, I confirm and

republish my Last Will and Testament as referred to

above on this the _____ day of _____ 19_____ .

_____

(your signature)

☑ *Also Include the Witnesses' Attestation Clause:*

This codicil was signed, published and declared by

_____ on _____
(your name)   (date)

in the presence of all of us. At his/her request and in

his/her presence and in the presence of each other, we

now sign as witnesses and declare that to the best of our

knowledge he/she appeared to be of legal age, of sound

mind and memory and under no constraint or undue

influence at the time he/she executed this codicil. We

declare this to be true under penalty of perjury.

_____
(signature and address of witness)

_____
(signature and address of witness)

_____
(signature and address of witness)

Self-Proving Affidavit for Codicils

The self-proving affidavit for your codicil is drafted and executed in the same manner as the self-proving affidavit you executed for your original will. Fill in this form to prepare a self-proving affidavit for your codicil.

Self-Proving Affidavit

STATE OF _____

COUNTY OF _____

Clause Continued on Following Page

We, _____,

_____,

_____ and

_____,

the testator and witnesses respectively, whose names

are signed to the attached codicil, being first duly sworn,

do declare to the undersigned officer that the testator

declared, signed and executed the foregoing instrument

as his/her First Codicil to his/her Last Will and Testament;

signed willingly (or willingly directed another to sign for

him/her); executed the codicil as his/her free and

voluntary act for the purposes therein expressed. We

also declare that each of the witnesses, in the presence

of the testator and at his/her request and in the presence

of each other, signed the codicil as a witness and that to

the best of his/her knowledge the testator was at the

time of legal age, of sound mind and memory and under

no constraint or undue influence at the time he/she

executed the codicil.

Clause Continued on Following Page

(signature of testator)

(signature and address of witness)

(signature and address of witness)

(signature and address of witness)

Subscribed and sworn to before me by

_____,

the testator, and by _____,

_____ and _____,

the witnesses on this the _____ day of _____,

19 _____.

                              _____

                              Notary Public

(Seal)

                              My Commission Expires:

CONCLUSION

There are several "do-it-yourself" areas of law — and writing a will is certainly one of them. In no time at all, you can create a will that guarantees that your loved ones will receive what you want after you die. And if your estate-planning needs should change, you can easily update your will with a codicil, a new will or with other estate planning tools, like a trust.

Writing your will is easy and inexpensive. Don't put it off because you don't want to pay a lawyer or think you're too young or too poor to have to worry about your possessions. With a few simple steps, you can organize your estate and literally rest in peace.

APPENDICES

STATE LAWS RELATING TO WILLS

The following listing contains a compilation of state laws relating to wills for all fifty states and the District of Columbia. It is recommended that you review the listing which pertains to your home state and any state in which you own real estate before you complete your will. The will clauses used in this book are generally designed to overcome and eliminate most potential legal problems raised by any of these individual state laws. There may, however, be some information which will directly affect the manner in which you decide to prepare your will.

As you review your state's particular laws, keep in mind that your will is going to be interpreted under the laws of the state in which you reside at the time of your death. Your personal property will be distributed according to the laws of the state in which you were a resident at the time of your death. Your real estate, however, will be distributed under the laws of the state in which it is located, regardless of where you are a resident.

Every effort has been made to insure that this list is as complete and up-to-date as possible. However, state laws are subject to change. While most laws relating to wills are relatively stable, it is advisable to check your particular state statutes to be certain there have been no major modifications since this book was prepared. To simplify this process as much as possible, the statute book description of each state's laws has been included in the following list. By using this description, you may easily locate the appropriate laws at your local library. If you have any difficulty, your local librarian will be glad to help.

Be forewarned, however, that most legislators are lawyers and that, therefore, much of your state's statutes will be written in a difficult-to-understand legal jargon. Use the Glossary in Appendix VI to translate this language.

The state-by-state listings in this Appendix contain the following information for each state:

State Law Description

This listing contains a brief description of the state law book and chapter or section number listing where most of the relevant state laws on wills and probate are contained.

Court With Probate Jurisdiction

This listing provides the name of the particular court in each state which has exclusive jurisdiction over probate and will-related legal matters.

Minimum Age for Disposing of Property by Will

This listing details the minimum age for having a legally valid will. For most states, this age is 18, but there are a few states that have differing laws.

Required Number of Witnesses

For most states, the minimum number of required witnesses is two. Be advised, however, that it is recommended to use at least three witnesses for your will.

May Witnesses Be Beneficiaries?

Under this listing is information regarding whether witnesses to the signing of the will may be beneficiaries under the will. Again, be advised that, to be safe, your witnesses should not be beneficiaries.

Are There Provisions for Self-Proving Wills?

This listing details whether there are specific state law provisions for self-proving wills. Only three states (Ohio, Vermont and Wisconsin), and the District of Columbia do not have a statutory provision for self-proved wills. To be prudent, however, everyone (including residents of Ohio, Vermont, Wisconsin and the District of Columbia) is advised to draft a Self-Proving Affidavit for their will. This listing explains if you can use the affidavit provided on page 110 or if a locally-prepared affidavit is more advisable.

Are Living Wills Recognized?

Under this listing, the name of any relevant state laws regarding living wills is shown. However, for residents in those few states that have not yet enacted laws recognizing living wills, it is still recommended that you prepare one. State-specific living will and durable power of attorney for health care forms are available for free from, *Choice In Dying*, 200 Varick St., New York, NY 10014.

How Does Divorce Affect the Will?

The effect of divorce on the will under state law is shown in this listing. State law varies widely on this point, and in some states, a divorce may automatically revoke your entire will. It is highly recommended that you review and update your will if you are ever divorced.

How Does Marriage Affect the Will?

This listing provides the state law on the effect of marriage on the will. Again, state law provides various provisions and marriage may have the drastic effect of entirely revoking your will. It is,

therefore, recommended that you review and
update your will if you are ever married.

Who Must Be Mentioned in the Will?

Under this listing is shown which parties must
be specifically mentioned in the will. Certain
parties must be mentioned in your will or they
may be entitled to an intestate share of your estate
regardless of your will. Most states provide this
protection for children born after a will is made
and for new spouses from a marriage that takes
place after a will is prepared. However, it is
recommended that you review and change your
will if you adopt or have any new children, are
married, or if any of your named beneficiaries die.

Spouse's Right to Property Regardless of Will

This listing provides the results of a spouse's
right of election against the will. In all states, the
surviving spouse has a right to a certain share of
the deceased spouse's estate regardless of any
provisions in the will of the deceased spouse
which may give him or her less than this
"statutory" or "community" property share.

Laws of Intestate Distribution (Distribution If Decedent Leaves No Will)

Under this listing, the complex state provisions
regarding intestate distribution of estates are
outlined. This provides an overview of how your
property would be distributed in the event that you
die without a valid will. The laws in this area are
extremely complex and differ widely from state to
state. The outline of laws shown in this listing is
intended to provide a simplified example of the
particular state distribution scheme. If specific
details of your state's distribution plan are needed,
please consult the state statute directly.

A definition of *life estate* may be useful in deciphering the information listed in this section. A life estate in real estate is provided to the surviving spouse in some states upon a spouse's death. A life estate means that the surviving spouse has the full use and enjoyment of any real estate for her or his entire life. However, upon her or his death, the property will pass automatically to the person who has the remaining share of the estate. Most often this will be a child of the original deceased. The spouse who is given a life estate can not leave such a property interest to anyone else.

Forms of Property Ownership?
This listing notes the types of property ownership recognized by your state and whether your state follows the community property or common law system for marital property.

State Restrictions on Gifts to Charities?
This listing notes whether the state has restrictions on after-death gifts to charities. If your state has such restrictions, and you are contemplating a significant gift to a church or charity, please consult with an attorney.

State Gift, Inheritance or Estate Taxes
This listing shows the tax situation in each state as it relates to estates and wills. There are three basic taxes that apply: gift taxes, inheritance taxes, and estate taxes. Each individual state may impose any of these taxes. Only one state, Nevada, does not impose any of these taxes.

ALABAMA

State Law Description: Code of Alabama; Title 43, Chapters 2-1 to 8-298.

Court With Probate Jurisdiction: Probate Court.

Minimum Age for Disposing of Property by Will: 18 for personal property, 19 for real estate.

Required Number of Witnesses: Two. (Three recommended.)

May Witnesses Be Beneficiaries?: Yes. (Not recommended.)

Are There Provisions for Self-Proving Wills?: Yes. (Use the Self-Proving Affidavit in Chapter 13.)

Are Living Wills Recognized?: Yes, under the "Alabama Natural Death Act."

How Does Divorce Affect the Will?: Revokes the will as to the divorced spouse.

How Does Marriage Affect the Will?: Revokes the will as to the spouse if she or he is not otherwise provided for. Spouse may still be entitled to her or his statutory share under the state intestate laws.

Who Must Be Mentioned in the Will?: Children, born or adopted; surviving spouse.

Spouse's Right to Property Regardless of Will: The surviving spouse is entitled to 1/3 of the "augmented" estate of the deceased spouse. In general, the "augmented" estate includes both the property that passes under the will and any other property that passes by other "non-will" transfers, such as under the terms of a living trust or a joint tenancy arrangement.

Laws of Intestate Distribution (Distribution If Decedent Leaves No Will):

Spouse and Children of Spouse Surviving: $50,000 and 1/2 of balance of estate to spouse and 1/2 of balance to children.

Spouse and Children Not of Spouse Surviving: 1/2 to spouse and 1/2 to children.

Spouse, but No Children or Parent(s) Surviving: All to spouse.

Spouse and Parent(s), but No Children Surviving: $100,000 and 1/2 of balance to spouse and 1/2 of balance to parent(s).

Children, but No Spouse Surviving: All to children equally or to their children per stirpes.

Parent(s), but No Spouse or Children Surviving: All to parents equally or the surviving parent.

No Spouse, Children or Parent(s) Surviving: All to brothers and sisters per stirpes; then to grandparents or their children per stirpes; then to deceased spouse's next of kin.

Forms of Property Ownership: Common law state. Tenancy in common presumed if real estate is held jointly, unless title creates joint tenancy with "right of survivorship" or similar words. No tenancy in entirety.

State Restrictions on Gifts to Charities?: No.

State Gift, Inheritance or Estate Taxes: No gift tax; no inheritance tax; imposes state estate tax equal to federal credit for state death taxes.

ALASKA

State Law Description: Alaska Statutes; Sections 13.06 +.
Court With Probate Jurisdiction: Superior Court.
Minimum Age for Disposing of Property by Will: 18.
Required Number of Witnesses: Two. (Three recommended.)
May Witnesses Be Beneficiaries?: Yes. (Not recommended.)
Are There Provisions for Self-Proving Wills?: Yes. (Use the Affidavit in Chapter 13.)
Are Living Wills Recognized?: Yes, under the "Alaska Rights of Terminally Ill Act."
How Does Divorce Affect the Will?: Revokes the will as to the divorced spouse.
How Does Marriage Affect the Will?: Revokes the will as to the spouse if she or he is not otherwise provided for. Spouse may still be entitled to her or his statutory share under the state intestate laws.
Who Must Be Mentioned in the Will?: Children, born or adopted; surviving spouse.
Spouse's Right to Property Regardless of Will: The surviving spouse is entitled to 1/3 of the "augmented" estate of the deceased spouse. In general, the "augmented" estate includes both the property that passes under the will and any other property that passes by other "non-will" transfers, such as under the terms of a living trust or a joint tenancy arrangement.
Laws of Intestate Distribution (Distribution If Decedent Leaves No Will):
  Spouse and Children of Spouse Surviving: $50,000 and 1/2 of balance to spouse and 1/2 of balance to children or grandchildren per stirpes.
  Spouse and Children Not of Spouse Surviving: 1/2 to spouse and 1/2 to children or grandchildren per stirpes.
  Spouse, but No Children or Parent(s) Surviving: All to spouse.
  Spouse and Parent(s), but No Children Surviving: $50,000 and 1/2 of balance to spouse and 1/2 of balance to parents.
  Children, but No Spouse Surviving: All to children equally or to their children per stirpes.
  Parent(s), but No Spouse or Children Surviving: All to parents equally, or to the surviving parent.
  No Spouse, Children or Parent(s) Surviving: All to brothers and sisters per stirpes; or if none, 1/2 to paternal grandparents and their children per stirpes and 1/2 to maternal grandparents and their children per stirpes.
Forms of Property Ownership: Common law state. No joint tenancy in personal property. Persons with undivided interests in real estate are tenants in common. Spouses who acquire real estate hold it as tenants by entirety unless stated otherwise.
State Restrictions on Gifts to Charities?: No.
State Gift, Inheritance or Estate Taxes: No gift tax; no inheritance tax; imposes state estate tax equal to federal credit for state death taxes.

ARIZONA

State Law Description: Arizona Revised Statutes Annotated; Title 14, Chapters 1102+, Title 33, Chapters 601+.
Court With Probate Jurisdiction: Superior Court.
Minimum Age for Disposing of Property by Will: 18.
Required Number of Witnesses: Two. (Three recommended.)
May Witnesses Be Beneficiaries?: Yes. (Not recommended.)
Are There Provisions for Self-Proving Wills?: Yes. (Use the Affidavit in Chapter 13.)
Are Living Wills Recognized?: Yes, under the "Arizona Medical Treatment Decision Act."
How Does Divorce Affect the Will?: Revokes the will as to the divorced spouse.
How Does Marriage Affect the Will?: Revokes the will as to the spouse if she or he is not otherwise provided for. Spouse may still be entitled to her or his statutory share under the state intestate laws.
Who Must Be Mentioned in the Will?: Children, born or adopted; surviving spouse.
Spouse's Right to Property Regardless of Will: Community property right to 1/2 of the deceased spouse's "community" property.
Laws of Intestate Distribution (Distribution If Decedent Leaves No Will):
  Spouse and Children of Spouse Surviving: All of decedent's separate property and 1/2 of decedent's community property to spouse and 1/2 of decedent's community property to children.
  Spouse and Children Not of Spouse Surviving: 1/2 of decedent's separate property to spouse and 1/2 of decedent's separate property and all of decedents community property to children.
  Spouse, but No Children or Parent(s) Surviving: All to spouse.
  Spouse and Parent(s), but No Children Surviving: All to spouse.
  Children, but No Spouse Surviving: All to children equally or to their children per stirpes.
  Parent(s), but No Spouse or Children Surviving: All to parents equally, or to the surviving parent.
  No Spouse, Children or Parent(s) Surviving: All to brothers and sisters per stirpes; or if none, to the next of kin.
Forms of Property Ownership: Community property state. Property acquired during marriage outside state before moving into state is quasi-community property controlled by Arizona law. Joint tenancy between spouses if stated. No tenancy by entirety.
State Restrictions on Gifts to Charities?: No.
State Gift, Inheritance or Estate Taxes: No gift tax; no inheritance tax; imposes state estate tax equal to federal credit for state death taxes.

ARKANSAS

State Law Description: Arkansas Code of 1987 Annotated; Title 28, Chapters 24-101 to 48-305.
Court With Probate Jurisdiction: Probate Court.
Minimum Age for Disposing of Property by Will: 18.
Required Number of Witnesses: Two. (Three recommended.)
May Witnesses Be Beneficiaries?: No.
Are There Provisions for Self-Proving Wills?: Yes. (Use the Affidavit in Chapter 13.)
Are Living Wills Recognized?: Yes, under the "Arkansas Rights of the Terminally Ill or Permanently Unconscious Act."
How Does Divorce Affect the Will?: Revokes the will as to the divorced spouse.
How Does Marriage Affect the Will?: Does not revoke the will.
Who Must Be Mentioned in the Will?: Children, born or adopted; surviving spouse.
Spouse's Right to Property Regardless of Will: Intestate share: 1/3 of personal property and 1/3 of real estate for life.
Laws of Intestate Distribution (Distribution If Decedent Leaves No Will):
    Spouse and Children of Spouse Surviving: Real estate: 1/3 life estate to spouse and 2/3 to children equally or their children per stirpes; personal property: 1/3 to spouse and 2/3 to children equally or their children per stirpes.
    Spouse and Children Not of Spouse Surviving: Real estate: 1/3 life estate to spouse and 2/3 to children equally or their children per stirpes; personal property: 1/3 to spouse and 2/3 to children equally or their children per stirpes.
    Spouse, but No Children or Parent(s) Surviving: All to spouse if married over 3 years. If married less than 3 years, 1/2 to spouse and 1/2 to brothers and sisters equally or their children per stirpes; or if none, then to ancestors (up to great- grandparents; or if none, all to spouse).
    Spouse and Parent(s), but No Children Surviving: All to spouse if married over 3 years. If married less than 3 years, 1/2 to spouse and 1/2 to parent(s).
    Children, but No Spouse Surviving: All to children equally or to their children per stirpes.
    Parent(s), but No Spouse or Children Surviving: All to parents equally, or to the surviving parent.
    No Spouse, Children or Parent(s) Surviving: All to brothers and sisters per stirpes; or if none, to grandparents, and their children per stirpes.
Forms of Property Ownership: Common law state. Property acquired in another state is community property if considered so in other state. Tenancy in common, joint tenancy recognized. Tenancy by entirety recognized when conveyed to husband and wife.
State Restrictions on Gifts to Charities?: No.
State Gift, Inheritance or Estate Taxes: No gift tax; no inheritance tax; imposes state estate tax equal to federal credit for state death taxes.

CALIFORNIA

State Law Description: Annotated California Code; Probate Code; Sections 6100+.

Court With Probate Jurisdiction: Superior Court.

Minimum Age for Disposing of Property by Will: 18.

Required Number of Witnesses: Two. (Three recommended.)

May Witnesses Be Beneficiaries?: No.

Are There Provisions for Self-Proving Wills?: Yes. (Use the Affidavit in Chapter 13.)

Are Living Wills Recognized?: Yes, under the "California Natural Death Act."

How Does Divorce Affect the Will?: Does not revoke the will.

How Does Marriage Affect the Will?: Revokes the will as to the surviving spouse.

Who Must Be Mentioned in the Will?: Children, born or adopted; grandchildren (if of deceased child); surviving spouse.

Spouse's Right to Property Regardless of Will: Community property right to 1/2 of the deceased spouse's "community" property.

Laws of Intestate Distribution (Distribution If Decedent Leaves No Will):

Spouse and Children of Spouse Surviving: All of decedent's community property to spouse. If one child: 1/2 of decedent's separate property to spouse and 1/2 to child per stirpes. If more than one child: 1/3 of decedent's separate property to spouse and 2/3 to children per stirpes.

Spouse and Children Not of Spouse Surviving: Same as above "Spouse and Children of Spouse Surviving."

Spouse, but No Children or Parent(s) Surviving: All of decedent's community property to spouse. 1/2 of decedent's separate property to spouse and 1/2 of decedent's separate property to brothers and sisters equally or to their children per stirpes; or if none, all to spouse.

Spouse and Parent(s), but No Children Surviving: All of decedent's community property to spouse. 1/2 of decedent's separate property to spouse and 1/2 of decedent's separate property to parent(s) or surviving parent.

Children, but No Spouse Surviving: All to children equally or to their children per stirpes.

Parent(s), but No Spouse or Children Surviving: All to parents equally, or to the surviving parent.

No Spouse, Children or Parent(s) Surviving: All to brothers and sisters per stirpes; or if none, to the next of kin.

Forms of Property Ownership: Community property state. Property in names of spouses as joint tenants is not community property unless stated. Joint tenancy must be stated. No tenancy by entirety.

State Restrictions on Gifts to Charities?: No.

State Gift, Inheritance or Estate Taxes: No gift tax; no inheritance tax; imposes state estate tax equal to federal credit for state death taxes.

Note: Fill-in-the-blank statutory will forms available from probate court and legal stationery stores.

COLORADO

State Law Description: Colorado Revised Statutes Annotated; Sections 15-10-101+, 15-11-101+, 15-12-101+.
Court With Probate Jurisdiction: District Court. (Probate Court in Denver.)
Minimum Age for Disposing of Property by Will: 18.
Required Number of Witnesses: Two. (Three recommended.)
May Witnesses Be Beneficiaries?: Yes. (Not recommended.)
Are There Provisions for Self-Proving Wills?: Yes. (Use the Affidavit in Chapter 13.)
Are Living Wills Recognized?: Yes, under the "Colorado Medical Treatment Decision Act."
How Does Divorce Affect the Will?: Revokes the will as to the divorced spouse.
How Does Marriage Affect the Will?: Revokes the will as to the spouse if she or he is not otherwise provided for. Spouse may still be entitled to her or his statutory share under the state intestate laws.
Who Must Be Mentioned in the Will?: Children, born or adopted; surviving spouse.
Spouse's Right to Property Regardless of Will: The surviving spouse is entitled to 1/2 of the "augmented" estate of the deceased spouse. In general, the "augmented" estate includes both the property that passes under the will and any other property that passes by other "non-will" transfers, such as under the terms of a living trust or a joint tenancy arrangement.
Laws of Intestate Distribution (Distribution If Decedent Leaves No Will):
  Spouse and Children of Spouse Surviving: $25,000 and 1/2 of balance to spouse and 1/2 of balance to children and grandchildren per stirpes.
  Spouse and Children Not of Spouse Surviving: 1/2 to spouse and 1/2 to children and grandchildren per stirpes.
  Spouse, but No Children or Parent(s) Surviving: All to spouse.
  Spouse and Parent(s), but No Children Surviving: All to spouse.
  Children, but No Spouse Surviving: All to children equally or to their children per stirpes.
  Parent(s), but No Spouse or Children Surviving: All to parents equally, or to the surviving parent.
  No Spouse, Children or Parent(s) Surviving: All to brothers and sisters per stirpes; or if none, to grandparents and their children per stirpes; or if none, to nearest lineal ancestors and their children.
Forms of Property Ownership: Common law state. Tenancy in common presumed unless otherwise stated. Joint tenancy recognized. No tenancy by entirety.
State Restrictions on Gifts to Charities?: No.
State Gift, Inheritance or Estate Taxes: No gift tax; no inheritance tax; imposes state estate tax equal to federal credit for state death taxes.

CONNECTICUT

State Law Description: Connecticut General Statutes Annotated; Title 45, Chapters 1+, 160+, 230b+.
Court With Probate Jurisdiction: Probate Court.
Minimum Age for Disposing of Property by Will: 18.
Required Number of Witnesses: Two. (Three recommended.)
May Witnesses Be Beneficiaries?: No.
Are There Provisions for Self-Proving Wills?: Yes. (Use the Affidavit in Chapter 13.)
Are Living Wills Recognized?: Yes, under the "Connecticut Removal of Life Support Systems Act."
How Does Divorce Affect the Will?: Revokes the will completely.
How Does Marriage Affect the Will?: Revokes the will completely.
Who Must Be Mentioned in the Will?: Children, born or adopted; surviving spouse.
Spouse's Right to Property Regardless of Will: The surviving spouse is entitled to 1/3 of the deceased spouse's real estate for the rest of his or her life.
Laws of Intestate Distribution (Distribution If Decedent Leaves No Will):
   Spouse and Children of Spouse Surviving: $100,000 and 1/2 of balance to spouse and 1/2 of balance to children or grandchildren per stirpes.
   Spouse and Children Not of Spouse Surviving: 1/2 to spouse and 1/2 to children or grandchildren per stirpes.
   Spouse, but No Children or Parent(s) Surviving: All to spouse.
   Spouse and Parent(s), but No Children Surviving: $100,000 and 3/4 of balance to spouse, 1/4 of balance to parents or surviving parent.
   Children, but No Spouse Surviving: All to children equally or to their children per stirpes.
   Parent(s), but No Spouse or Children Surviving: All to parents equally, or to the surviving parent.
   No Spouse, Children or Parent(s) Surviving: All to brothers and sisters per stirpes; or if none, to next of kin.
Forms of Property Ownership: Common law state. In joint ownership, tenancy in common presumed unless words "joint tenants" follow names. Joint tenancy automatically includes right of survivorship. No tenancy by entirety.
State Restrictions on Gifts to Charities?: No.
State Gift, Inheritance or Estate Taxes: No gift tax; no inheritance tax; imposes state estate tax equal to federal credit for state death taxes.

DELAWARE

State Law Description: Delaware Code Annotated; Title 12, Chapters 101+.
Court With Probate Jurisdiction: Chancery Court.
Minimum Age for Disposing of Property by Will: 18.
Required Number of Witnesses: Two. (Three recommended.)
May Witnesses Be Beneficiaries?: Yes. (Not recommended.)
Are There Provisions for Self-Proving Wills?: Yes. (Use the Affidavit in Chapter 13.)
Are Living Wills Recognized?: Yes, under the "Delaware Death With Dignity Act."
How Does Divorce Affect the Will?: Revokes the will as to the divorced spouse.
How Does Marriage Affect the Will?: Does not revoke the will.
Who Must Be Mentioned in the Will?: Children, born or adopted; surviving spouse.
Spouse's Right to Property Regardless of Will: The surviving spouse is entitled to 1/3 of the deceased spouse's estate or $20,000.00, whichever is less.
Laws of Intestate Distribution (Distribution If Decedent Leaves No Will):
  Spouse and Children of Spouse Surviving: Real estate: Life estate to spouse; all the rest to children or grandchildren per stirpes; Personal property: $50,000 and 1/2 of balance to spouse and 1/2 of balance to children or grandchildren per stirpes.
  Spouse and Children Not of Spouse Surviving: Real estate: Life estate to spouse; all the rest to children or grandchildren per stirpes; Personal property: 1/2 to spouse and 1/2 to children or grandchildren per stirpes.
  Spouse, but No Children or Parent(s) Surviving: All to spouse.
  Spouse and Parent(s), but No Children Surviving: Real estate: Life estate to spouse; all the rest to parents or surviving parent; Personal property: $50,000 and 1/2 of balance to spouse and 1/2 of balance to parents or surviving parent.
  Children, but No Spouse Surviving: All to children equally or to their children per stirpes.
  Parent(s), but No Spouse or Children Surviving: All to parents equally, or to the surviving parent.
  No Spouse, Children or Parent(s) Surviving: All to brothers or sisters or their children per stirpes; or if none, to the next of kin.
Forms of Property Ownership: Common law state. Tenancy in common presumed. If joint owners are married, tenancy by entirety created. Joint tenancy created only if stated.
State Restrictions on Gifts to Charities?: No.
State Gift, Inheritance or Estate Taxes: Imposes a state gift tax; imposes an inheritance tax of up to 16%; imposes state estate tax equal to federal credit for state death taxes less any amounts paid on state inheritance tax. Maximum total state inheritance and state estate tax is equal to the maximum allowable federal estate tax credit for state death taxes.

DISTRICT OF COLUMBIA

State Law Description: District of Columbia Code Annotated;
Sections 16-101+, 18-101+, 20-101+, 45-101+.
Court With Probate Jurisdiction: Superior Court.
Minimum Age for Disposing of Property by Will: 18.
Required Number of Witnesses: Two. (Three recommended.)
May Witnesses Be Beneficiaries?: No.
Are There Provisions for Self-Proving Wills?: Not in statutes.
However self-proving affidavits have been accepted by courts. (Use
Affidavit in Chapter 13.)
Are Living Wills Recognized?: Yes, under the "District of Columbia
Natural Death Act."
How Does Divorce Affect the Will?: Generally, revokes the will.
How Does Marriage Affect the Will?: Generally, revokes the will.
Who Must Be Mentioned in the Will?: Surviving spouse.
Spouse's Right to Property Regardless of Will: The surviving
spouse is entitled to 1/3 of the deceased spouse's real estate for the
rest of his or her life.
*Laws of Intestate Distribution (Distribution If Decedent
Leaves No Will):*
  Spouse and Children of Spouse Surviving: Real estate: 1/3
  life estate to spouse and balance to children equally or their children
  per stirpes; Personal property: 1/3 to spouse and 2/3 to children
  equally or their children per stirpes.
  Spouse and Children Not of Spouse Surviving: Real
  estate: 1/3 life estate to spouse and balance to children equally or
  their children per stirpes; Personal property: 1/3 to spouse and 2/3 to
  children equally or their children per stirpes.
  Spouse, but No Children or Parent(s) Surviving: Real
  estate: 1/3 life estate to spouse and balance to parent's children per
  stirpes; or if none, to collaterals; or if none, to grandparents; or if
  none, all to spouse; Personal property: 1/2 to spouse and 1/2 to
  parent's children per stirpes; or if none, to collaterals; or if none, to
  grandparents; or if none, all to spouse.
  Spouse and Parent(s), but No Children Surviving: Real
  estate: 1/3 life estate to spouse and balance to parents or surviving
  parent; Personal property: 1/2 to spouse and 1/2 to parents or
  surviving parent.
  Children, but No Spouse Surviving: All to children equally or
  to their children per stirpes.
  Parent(s), but No Spouse or Children Surviving: All to
  parents equally, or to the surviving parent.
  No Spouse, Children or Parent(s) Surviving: All to brothers
  and sisters or their children per stirpes; or if none, to collaterals; or if
  none, to grandparents.
Forms of Property Ownership: Common law state. Tenancy in
common presumed unless joint tenancy stated. Joint tenancy, tenancy
by entirety can be created if at least one of the granting owners is also a
recipient owner. Joint ownership by husband and wife presumes
tenancy by entirety.
State Restrictions on Gifts to Charities?: No.

State Gift, Inheritance or Estate Taxes: No gift tax; no
inheritance tax; imposes state estate tax equal to federal credit for state
death taxes.

FLORIDA

State Law Description: Florida Statutes Annotated; Chapters 731.005+, 732.501+, 733.101+.
Court With Probate Jurisdiction: Circuit Court.
Minimum Age for Disposing of Property by Will: 18.
Required Number of Witnesses: Two. (Three recommended.)
May Witnesses Be Beneficiaries?: Yes. (Not recommended.)
Are There Provisions for Self-Proving Wills?: Yes. (Use the Affidavit in Chapter 13.)
Are Living Wills Recognized?: Yes, under the "Florida Life-Prolonging Procedure Act."
How Does Divorce Affect the Will?: Revokes the will as to the divorced spouse.
How Does Marriage Affect the Will?: Revokes the will as to the spouse if she or he is not otherwise provided for. Spouse may still be entitled to her or his statutory share under the state intestate laws.
Who Must Be Mentioned in the Will?: Children, born or adopted; surviving spouse.
Spouse's Right to Property Regardless of Will: The surviving spouse is entitled to 30% of the deceased spouse's estate.
Laws of Intestate Distribution (Distribution If Decedent Leaves No Will):
   Spouse and Children of Spouse Surviving: $20,000 and 1/2 of balance to spouse and 1/2 of balance to children and grandchildren per stirpes.
   Spouse and Children Not of Spouse Surviving: 1/2 to spouse and 1/2 to children and grandchildren per stirpes.
   Spouse, but No Children or Parent(s) Surviving: All to spouse.
   Spouse and Parent(s), but No Children Surviving: All to spouse.
   Children, but No Spouse Surviving: All to children equally or to their children per stirpes.
   Parent(s), but No Spouse or Children Surviving: All to parents equally, or to the surviving parent.
   No Spouse, Children or Parent(s) Surviving: All to brothers and sisters or their children per stirpes; or if none, 1/2 to maternal next of kin and 1/2 to paternal next of kin beginning with grandparents.
Forms of Property Ownership: Common law state. Personal property or real estate owned by husband and wife presumes tenancy by entirety and survivorship. Joint tenancy includes survivorship only if stated.
State Restrictions on Gifts to Charities?: Yes. If extensive gifts to charities are contemplated, please refer directly to statute or consult an attorney.
State Gift, Inheritance or Estate Taxes: No gift tax; no inheritance tax; imposes state estate tax equal to federal credit for state death taxes.

GEORGIA

State Law Description: Code of Georgia Annotated; Title 24, Sections 101+, Title 113, Sections 101+.

Court With Probate Jurisdiction: Probate Court.

Minimum Age for Disposing of Property by Will: 14.

Required Number of Witnesses: Two. (Three recommended.)

May Witnesses Be Beneficiaries?: No.

Are There Provisions for Self-Proving Wills?: Yes. (Use the Affidavit in Chapter 13.)

Are Living Wills Recognized?: Yes, under the "Georgia Living Wills Act."

How Does Divorce Affect the Will?: Revokes the will completely.

How Does Marriage Affect the Will?: Revokes the will completely.

Who Must Be Mentioned in the Will?: Statute contains detailed provisions regarding this matter. Please refer directly to statute text or consult an attorney if this is a critical factor.

Spouse's Right to Property Regardless of Will: The surviving spouse is entitled to one year's support from the deceased spouse's estate.

Laws of Intestate Distribution (Distribution If Decedent Leaves No Will):

   Spouse and Children of Spouse Surviving: Children or grandchildren and spouse all take equal shares, with at least 1/4 to spouse.

   Spouse and Children Not of Spouse Surviving: Children or grandchildren and spouse all take equal shares, with at least 1/4 to spouse.

   Spouse, but No Children or Parent(s) Surviving: All to spouse.

   Spouse and Parent(s), but No Children Surviving: All to spouse.

   Children, but No Spouse Surviving: All to children equally or to their children per stirpes.

   Parent(s), but No Spouse or Children Surviving: All to parents, brothers and sisters equally, or to their children per stirpes.

   No Spouse, Children or Parent(s) Surviving: All to brothers and sisters or their children per stirpes; or if none, to paternal and maternal next of kin.

Forms of Property Ownership: Common law state. Tenancy in common presumed unless ownership papers refer to "joint tenants" or similar language. No tenancy by entirety.

State Restrictions on Gifts to Charities?: Yes. If extensive gifts to charities are contemplated, please refer directly to statute or consult an attorney.

State Gift, Inheritance or Estate Taxes: No gift tax; no inheritance tax; imposes state estate tax equal to federal credit for state death taxes.

HAWAII

State Law Description: Hawaii Revised Statutes; Title 560, Sections 2+.

Court With Probate Jurisdiction: Circuit Court.

Minimum Age for Disposing of Property by Will: 18.

Required Number of Witnesses: Two. (Three recommended.)

May Witnesses Be Beneficiaries?: Yes. (Not recommended.)

Are There Provisions for Self-Proving Wills?: Yes. (Use the Affidavit in Chapter 13.)

Are Living Wills Recognized?: Yes, under the "Hawaii Medical Treatment Decisions Act."

How Does Divorce Affect the Will?: Revokes the will as to the divorced spouse.

How Does Marriage Affect the Will?: Revokes the will as to the spouse if she or he is not otherwise provided for. Spouse may still be entitled to her or his statutory share under the state intestate laws.

Who Must Be Mentioned in the Will?: Children, born or adopted; surviving spouse.

Spouse's Right to Property Regardless of Will: The surviving spouse is entitled to 1/3 of the deceased spouse's estate.

Laws of Intestate Distribution (Distribution If Decedent Leaves No Will):

   Spouse and Children of Spouse Surviving: 1/2 to spouse and 1/2 to children equally or to the grandchildren.

   Spouse and Children Not of Spouse Surviving: 1/2 to spouse and 1/2 to children equally or to the grandchildren.

   Spouse, but No Children or Parent(s) Surviving: All to spouse.

   Spouse and Parent(s), but No Children Surviving: 1/2 to spouse and 1/2 to parents or surviving parent.

   Children, but No Spouse Surviving: All to children equally or to their children per stirpes.

   Parent(s), but No Spouse or Children Surviving: All to parents equally, or to the surviving parent.

   No Spouse, Children or Parent(s) Surviving: All to brothers and sisters or their children per stirpes; or if none, to grandparents; or if none, to uncles and aunts equally.

Forms of Property Ownership: Common law state. Tenancy in common presumed unless stated as joint tenancy or tenancy by entirety.

State Restrictions on Gifts to Charities?: No.

State Gift, Inheritance or Estate Taxes: No gift tax; no inheritance tax; imposes state estate tax equal to federal credit for state death taxes.

IDAHO

State Law Description: Idaho Code (General Laws of Idaho Annotated); Title 15, Chapters 2-500+, 3-101+.
Court With Probate Jurisdiction: District Court.
Minimum Age for Disposing of Property by Will: 18, or emancipated from parents.
Required Number of Witnesses: Two. (Three recommended.)
May Witnesses Be Beneficiaries?: Yes. (Not recommended.)
Are There Provisions for Self-Proving Wills?: Yes. (Use the Affidavit in Chapter 13.)
Are Living Wills Recognized?: Yes, under the "Idaho Natural Death Act."
How Does Divorce Affect the Will?: Revokes the will as to the divorced spouse.
How Does Marriage Affect the Will?: Revokes the will as to the spouse if she or he is not otherwise provided for. Spouse may still be entitled to her or his statutory share under the state intestate laws.
Who Must Be Mentioned in the Will?: Children, born or adopted; surviving spouse.
Spouse's Right to Property Regardless of Will: Community property right to 1/2 of the deceased spouse's "community" property.
Laws of Intestate Distribution (Distribution If Decedent Leaves No Will):
    Spouse and Children of Spouse Surviving: All of decedent's community property to spouse; $50,000 and 1/2 of balance of decedent's separate property to spouse and 1/2 of balance to children or grandchildren per stirpes.
    Spouse and Children Not of Spouse Surviving: All of decedent's community property to spouse; 1/2 of decedent's separate property to spouse and 1/2 to children or grandchildren per stirpes.
    Spouse, but No Children or Parent(s) Surviving: All to spouse.
    Spouse and Parent(s), but No Children Surviving: All of decedent's community property to spouse; $50,000 and 1/2 of balance of decedent's separate property to spouse and 1/2 of balance to parents or surviving parent.
    Children, but No Spouse Surviving: All to children or to their children per stirpes.
    Parent(s), but No Spouse or Children Surviving: All to parents equally, or to the surviving parent.
    No Spouse, Children or Parent(s) Surviving: All to brothers and sisters or their children.
Forms of Property Ownership: Community property state. Tenancy in common presumed unless joint tenancy stated or property is acquired as partnership or community property. Tenancy by entirety not recognized.
State Restrictions on Gifts to Charities?: Yes. If extensive gifts to charities are contemplated, please refer directly to statute or consult an attorney.

State Gift, Inheritance or Estate Taxes: No gift tax; imposes an inheritance tax of up to 30%; imposes state estate tax equal to federal credit for state death taxes less any amounts paid on state inheritance tax. Maximum total state inheritance and state estate tax is equal to the maximum allowable federal estate tax credit for state death taxes.

ILLINOIS

State Law Description: Illinois Annotated Statutes; Chapter 25, Paragraphs 24+; Chapter 140 1/2, Paragraphs 1-1+.
Court With Probate Jurisdiction: Circuit Court.
Minimum Age for Disposing of Property by Will: 18.
Required Number of Witnesses: Two. (Three recommended.)
May Witnesses Be Beneficiaries?: No.
Are There Provisions for Self-Proving Wills?: Not in statutes. However self-proving affidavits have been accepted in the courts. (Use the Affidavit in Chapter 13.)
Are Living Wills Recognized?: Yes, under the "Illinois Living Will Act."
How Does Divorce Affect the Will?: Revokes the will as to the divorced spouse.
How Does Marriage Affect the Will?: Does not revoke the will.
Who Must Be Mentioned in the Will?: Children, born or adopted; surviving spouse.
Spouse's Right to Property Regardless of Will: Generally, the surviving spouse is entitled to 1/2 of the deceased spouse's estate if there are no children, and only 1/3 if there are children. However, please refer directly to the statute as the provisions are detailed.
Laws of Intestate Distribution (Distribution If Decedent Leaves No Will):
   Spouse and Children of Spouse Surviving: 1/2 to spouse and 1/2 to children equally or to the grandchildren per stirpes.
   Spouse and Children Not of Spouse Surviving: 1/2 to spouse and 1/2 to children equally or to the grandchildren per stirpes.
   Spouse, but No Children or Parent(s) Surviving: All to spouse.
   Spouse and Parent(s), but No Children Surviving: All to spouse.
   Children, but No Spouse Surviving: All to children equally or to their children per stirpes.
   Parent(s), but No Spouse or Children Surviving: All to parents, brothers, sisters, or children of brother and sisters per stirpes. If only one surviving parent, they take a double share.
   No Spouse, Children or Parent(s) Surviving: 1/2 to maternal and 1/2 to paternal grandparents equally or to surviving grandparent; or if none, to their children per stirpes; or if none, 1/2 to maternal and 1/2 to paternal great-grandparents equally or to surviving great-grandparent; or if none, to their children per stirpes; or if none of the above, all to the next of kin.
Forms of Property Ownership: Common law state. Tenancy in common presumed. Joint tenancy with right of survivorship created only by declaration that estate, including personal property, is in joint tenancy and not tenancy in common. Tenancy by entirety recognized.
State Restrictions on Gifts to Charities?: No.
State Gift, Inheritance or Estate Taxes: No gift tax; no inheritance tax; imposes state estate tax equal to federal credit for state death taxes.

INDIANA

State Law Description: Indiana Code Annotated; Title 29, Chapters 1-1+.

Court With Probate Jurisdiction: Circuit or Superior Court. (Probate Court in St. Joseph and Vigo Counties.)

Minimum Age for Disposing of Property by Will: 18, or member of Armed Forces or Merchant Marines.

Required Number of Witnesses: Two. (Three recommended.)

May Witnesses Be Beneficiaries?: No.

Are There Provisions for Self-Proving Wills?: Yes. (Use the Affidavit in Chapter 13.)

Are Living Wills Recognized?: Yes, under the "Indiana Living Wills and Life-Prolonging Procedures Act."

How Does Divorce Affect the Will?: Revokes the will as to the divorced spouse.

How Does Marriage Affect the Will?: Does not revoke the will.

Who Must Be Mentioned in the Will?: Children, born or adopted; surviving spouse.

Spouse's Right to Property Regardless of Will: The surviving spouse is entitled to 1/3 of the deceased spouse's estate.

Laws of Intestate Distribution (Distribution If Decedent Leaves No Will):

Spouse and Children of Spouse Surviving: If one child, 1/2 to spouse and 1/2 to child; if more than one child, 1/3 to spouse and 2/3 to children.

Spouse and Children Not of Spouse Surviving: Real estate: life estate to spouse, balance to children; Personal property: if one child, 1/2 to spouse and 1/2 to child; if more than one child, 1/3 to spouse and 2/3 to children.

Spouse, but No Children or Parent(s) Surviving: All to spouse.

Spouse and Parent(s), but No Children Surviving: 3/4 to spouse and 1/4 to parents or surviving parent.

Children, but No Spouse Surviving: All to children equally or to their children per stirpes.

Parent(s), but No Spouse or Children Surviving: 1/2 to parents if both surviving, 1/2 to brothers and sisters and their children per stirpes; if only one parent surviving, then 1/4 to parent and 3/4 to brothers and sisters and their children per stirpes.

No Spouse, Children or Parent(s) Surviving: All to brothers and sisters or their children per stirpes; or if none, to grandparents; or if none, to aunts and uncles per stirpes.

Forms of Property Ownership: Common law state. Joint tenancy, tenancy in common and tenancy by entirety recognized. For real estate jointly owned (except by married couples), tenancy in common presumed unless joint tenancy stated. Joint ownership by husband and wife presumes tenancy by entirety.

State Restrictions on Gifts to Charities?: No.

State Gift, Inheritance or Estate Taxes: No gift tax; imposes an inheritance tax of up to 20%; imposes state estate tax equal to federal credit for state death taxes less any amounts paid on state inheritance tax. Maximum total state inheritance and state estate tax is equal to the maximum allowable federal estate tax credit for state death taxes.

IOWA

State Law Description: Iowa Code Annotated; Sections 633.1+.
Court With Probate Jurisdiction: District Court.
Minimum Age for Disposing of Property by Will: 18.
Required Number of Witnesses: Two. (Three recommended.)
May Witnesses Be Beneficiaries?: No.
Are There Provisions for Self-Proving Wills?: Yes. (Use the Affidavit in Chapter 13.)
Are Living Wills Recognized?: Yes, under the "Iowa Life-Sustaining Procedures Act."
How Does Divorce Affect the Will?: Generally does not revoke the will.
How Does Marriage Affect the Will?: Revokes the will as to the spouse if she or he is not otherwise provided for. Spouse may still be entitled to her or his statutory share under the state intestate laws.
Who Must Be Mentioned in the Will?: Children, born or adopted; surviving spouse.
Spouse's Right to Property Regardless of Will: The surviving spouse is entitled to 1/3 of the deceased spouse's estate.
Laws of Intestate Distribution (Distribution If Decedent Leaves No Will):
   Spouse and Children of Spouse Surviving: All to spouse.
   Spouse and Children Not of Spouse Surviving: $50,000 and 1/2 of balance to spouse and 1/2 of balance to children.
   Spouse, but No Children or Parent(s) Surviving: All to spouse.
   Spouse and Parent(s), but No Children Surviving: All to spouse.
   Children, but No Spouse Surviving: All to children equally or to their children per stirpes.
   Parent(s), but No Spouse or Children Surviving: All to parents equally, or to the surviving parent.
   No Spouse, Children or Parent(s) Surviving: All to brothers and sisters or their children per stirpes; or if none, to ancestors and their children per stirpes; or if none, to heirs of deceased.
Forms of Property Ownership: Common law state. Tenancy in common presumed unless joint tenancy stated. No tenancy by entirety.
State Restrictions on Gifts to Charities?: No.
State Gift, Inheritance or Estate Taxes: No gift tax; imposes an inheritance tax of up to 15%; imposes state estate tax equal to federal credit for state death taxes less any amounts paid on state inheritance tax. Maximum total state inheritance and state estate tax is equal to the maximum allowable federal estate tax credit for state death taxes.

KANSAS

State Law Description: Kansas Statutes Annotated; Chapter 79, Subjects Sections -101, 501+, 601+.

Court With Probate Jurisdiction: District Court.

Minimum Age for Disposing of Property by Will: 18.

Required Number of Witnesses: Two. (Three recommended.)

May Witnesses Be Beneficiaries?: Yes. (Not recommended.)

Are There Provisions for Self-Proving Wills?: Yes. (Use the Affidavit in Chapter 13.)

Are Living Wills Recognized?: Yes, under the "Kansas Natural Death Act."

How Does Divorce Affect the Will?: Revokes the will as to the divorced spouse.

How Does Marriage Affect the Will?: Revokes the will if a child is later born to or adopted into the marriage.

Who Must Be Mentioned in the Will?: Surviving spouse.

Spouse's Right to Property Regardless of Will: Generally, the surviving spouse is entitled to 1/2 of the deceased spouse's estate if there are no children, and only 1/3 if there are children. However, please refer directly to the statute as the provisions are detailed.

Laws of Intestate Distribution (Distribution If Decedent Leaves No Will):

   Spouse and Children of Spouse Surviving: 1/2 to spouse and 1/2 to children or grandchildren per stirpes.

   Spouse and Children Not of Spouse Surviving: 1/2 to spouse and 1/2 to children or grandchildren per stirpes.

   Spouse, but No Children or Parent(s) Surviving: All to spouse.

   Spouse and Parent(s), but No Children Surviving: All to spouse.

   Children, but No Spouse Surviving: All to children equally or to their children per stirpes.

   Parent(s), but No Spouse or Children Surviving: All to parents equally, or to the surviving parent.

   No Spouse, Children or Parent(s) Surviving: All to brothers and sisters per stirpes.

Forms of Property Ownership: Common law state. Tenancy in common presumed unless joint tenancy stated and transfer is from sole owner to himself or herself and one other. No tenancy by entirety.

State Restrictions on Gifts to Charities?: No.

State Gift, Inheritance or Estate Taxes: No gift tax; imposes an inheritance tax of up to 15%; imposes state estate tax equal to federal credit for state death taxes less any amounts paid on state inheritance tax. Maximum total state inheritance and state estate tax is equal to the maximum allowable federal estate tax credit for state death taxes.

KENTUCKY

State Law Description: Kentucky Revised Statutes; Chapters 394.000+, 395.000+.

Court With Probate Jurisdiction: District Court.

Minimum Age for Disposing of Property by Will: 18.

Required Number of Witnesses: Two. (Three recommended.)

May Witnesses Be Beneficiaries?: No.

Are There Provisions for Self-Proving Wills?: Yes. (Use the Affidavit in Chapter 13.)

Are Living Wills Recognized?: Yes, under the "Kentucky Living Will Act."

How Does Divorce Affect the Will?: Revokes the will as to the divorced spouse.

How Does Marriage Affect the Will?: Revokes the will completely.

Who Must Be Mentioned in the Will?: Children, born or adopted; surviving spouse.

Spouse's Right to Property Regardless of Will: The surviving spouse is entitled to 1/3 of the deceased spouse's real estate for the rest of his or her life.

Laws of Intestate Distribution (Distribution If Decedent Leaves No Will):

Spouse and Children of Spouse Surviving: Real estate: life estate of 1/3 of fee simple property acquired during marriage and 1/2 of other real estate to spouse; balance to children or grandchildren per stirpes; Personal property: 1/2 to spouse and 1/2 to children equally or grandchildren per stirpes.

Spouse and Children Not of Spouse Surviving: Same as above for "Spouse and Children of Spouse Surviving."

Spouse, but No Children or Parent(s) Surviving: 1/2 to parents children; or if none, all to spouse.

Spouse and Parent(s), but No Children Surviving: 1/2 to spouse and 1/2 to parents or surviving parent.

Children, but No Spouse Surviving: All to children equally or to their children per stirpes.

Parent(s), but No Spouse or Children Surviving: All to parents equally, or to the surviving parent.

No Spouse, Children or Parent(s) Surviving: All to brothers and sisters or their children per stirpes; or if none, 1/2 to maternal next of kin and 1/2 to paternal next of kin and their children per stirpes.

Forms of Property Ownership: Common law state. Tenancy in common presumed between husband and wife unless joint tenancy stated. Tenancy by entirety recognized.

State Restrictions on Gifts to Charities?: No.

State Gift, Inheritance or Estate Taxes: No gift tax; imposes an inheritance tax of up to 16%; imposes state estate tax equal to federal credit for state death taxes less any amounts paid on state inheritance tax. Maximum total state inheritance and state estate tax is equal to the maximum allowable federal estate tax credit for state death taxes.

LOUISIANA

State Law Description: Louisiana Revised Statutes; Louisiana Civil Code Annotated.

Court With Probate Jurisdiction: District Court.

Minimum Age for Disposing of Property by Will: 16.

Required Number of Witnesses: Three.

May Witnesses Be Beneficiaries?: No.

Are There Provisions for Self-Proving Wills?: Yes; however, use of a self-proving-affidavit is not necessary since the will itself must be notarized.

Are Living Wills Recognized?: Yes, under the "Louisiana Life-Sustaining Procedures Act."

How Does Divorce Affect the Will?: Does not revoke the will.

How Does Marriage Affect the Will?: Does not revoke the will.

Who Must Be Mentioned in the Will?: Children, born or adopted; surviving spouse.

Spouse's Right to Property Regardless of Will: The Louisiana Civil Code provisions regarding this matter are detailed and should be consulted directly.

Laws of Intestate Distribution (Distribution If Decedent Leaves No Will):

Spouse and Children of Spouse Surviving: All community property to descendants per stirpes. However, the spouse has the right to use the property until remarried. All separate property to children equally or grandchildren per stirpes.

Spouse and Children Not of Spouse Surviving: Same as above for "Spouse and Children of Spouse Surviving."

Spouse, but No Children or Parent(s) Surviving: All community property to spouse; all separate property to brothers and sisters or their children per stirpes; or if none, to parents; or if none, all to spouse.

Spouse and Parent(s), but No Children Surviving: All community property to spouse; all separate property to brothers and sisters or their children per stirpes; or if none, to parents; or if none, all to spouse.

Children, but No Spouse Surviving: All to children equally or to their children per stirpes.

Parent(s), but No Spouse or Children Surviving: All to parents equally, or to the surviving parent.

No Spouse, Children or Parent(s) Surviving: To brothers and sisters equally or their children per stirpes; or if none, to next of kin.

Forms of Property Ownership: Community property state. Joint ownership (called indivision) if two or more persons listed as owners. No tenancy by entirety or tenancy in common.

State Restrictions on Gifts to Charities?: No.

State Gift, Inheritance or Estate Taxes: Imposes a state gift tax; imposes an inheritance tax of up to 10%; imposes a state estate tax equal to federal credit for state death taxes less any amounts paid on state inheritance tax. Maximum total state inheritance and state estate tax is equal to the maximum allowable federal estate tax credit for state death taxes.

MAINE
State Law Description: Maine Revised Statutes Annotated; Title 18-A, Sections 1-101+, 2-501+, 3-101+.
Court With Probate Jurisdiction: Probate Court.
Minimum Age for Disposing of Property by Will: 18, married, or a surviving spouse.
Required Number of Witnesses: Three.
May Witnesses Be Beneficiaries?: Yes. (Not recommended.)
Are There Provisions for Self-Proving Wills?: Yes. (Use the Affidavit in Chapter 13.)
Are Living Wills Recognized?: Yes, under the "Maine Uniform Rights of the Terminally Ill Act."
How Does Divorce Affect the Will?: Revokes the will as to the divorced spouse.
How Does Marriage Affect the Will?: Revokes the will as to the spouse if she or he is not otherwise provided for. Spouse may still be entitled to her or his statutory share under the state intestate laws.
Who Must Be Mentioned in the Will?: Children, born or adopted; grandchildren (if of deceased child); surviving spouse.
Spouse's Right to Property Regardless of Will: The surviving spouse is entitled to 1/3 of the entire estate of the deceased spouse.
Laws of Intestate Distribution (Distribution If Decedent Leaves No Will):
  Spouse and Children of Spouse Surviving: $50,000 and 1/2 of balance to spouse and 1/2 of balance to children or grandchildren per stirpes.
  Spouse and Children Not of Spouse Surviving: 1/2 to spouse and 1/2 to children or grandchildren per stirpes.
  Spouse, but No Children or Parent(s) Surviving: $50,000 and 1/2 of balance to spouse and 1/2 of balance to parent's children per capita; or if none, 1/4 of balance to paternal and 1/4 to maternal grandparents or their children per capita.
  Spouse and Parent(s), but No Children Surviving: $50,000 and 1/2 of balance to spouse and 1/2 of balance to parents or surviving parent.
  Children, but No Spouse Surviving: All to children equally or to their children per stirpes.
  Parent(s), but No Spouse or Children Surviving: All to parents equally, or to the surviving parent.
  No Spouse, Children or Parent(s) Surviving: 1/2 to paternal grandparents or their children per capita and 1/2 to maternal grandparents or their children per capita.
Forms of Property Ownership: Common law state. Ownership by two or more presumes tenancy in common unless joint tenancy stated. No tenancy by entirety.
State Restrictions on Gifts to Charities?: No.
State Gift, Inheritance or Estate Taxes: No gift tax; no inheritance tax; imposes state estate tax equal to federal credit for state death taxes.
Note: Fill-in-the-blank statutory will forms available from probate court and legal stationery stores.

MARYLAND

State Law Description: Maryland Code; Estates and Trusts, Title 4, Sections 4-101+.

Court With Probate Jurisdiction: Orphan's Court. (Circuit Court in Harford and Montgomery Counties.)

Minimum Age for Disposing of Property by Will: 18.

Required Number of Witnesses: Two. (Three recommended.)

May Witnesses Be Beneficiaries?: Yes. (Not recommended.)

Are There Provisions for Self-Proving Wills?: Yes. (Use the Affidavit in Chapter 13.)

Are Living Wills Recognized?: Yes, under the "Maryland Life-Sustaining Procedures Act."

How Does Divorce Affect the Will?: Revokes the will as to the divorced spouse.

How Does Marriage Affect the Will?: Revokes the will if a child is later born to or adopted into the marriage and survives the maker of the will.

Who Must Be Mentioned in the Will?: Children, born or adopted; grandchildren (of deceased child); surviving spouse.

Spouse's Right to Property Regardless of Will: Generally, the surviving spouse is entitled to 1/2 of the deceased spouse's estate if there are no children, and only 1/3 if there are children. However, please refer directly to the statute for details.

Laws of Intestate Distribution (Distribution If Decedent Leaves No Will):

  Spouse and Children of Spouse Surviving: If any surviving children are minors, 1/2 to spouse and 1/2 to children equally or grandchildren per stirpes; if no surviving children are minors, $15,000 and 1/2 of balance to spouse and 1/2 of balance to children equally or grandchildren per stirpes.

  Spouse and Children Not of Spouse Surviving: Same as above for "Spouse and Children of Spouse Surviving."

  Spouse, but No Children or Parent(s) Surviving: All to spouse.

  Spouse and Parent(s), but No Children Surviving: 1/2 to spouse and 1/2 to parents or surviving parent.

  Children, but No Spouse Surviving: All to children or to their children per stirpes.

  Parent(s), but No Spouse or Children Surviving: All to parents equally, or to the surviving parent.

  No Spouse, Children or Parent(s) Surviving: All to brothers and sisters equally or to their children per stirpes; or if none, to collateral next of kin.

Forms of Property Ownership: Common law state. Tenancy in common recognized. Joint tenancy must be stated. Joint ownership by spouses presumes tenancy by entirety unless stated otherwise.

Restrictions on Gifts to Charities?: No.

State Gift, Inheritance or Estate Taxes: No gift tax; imposes an inheritance tax of up to 10%; imposes state estate tax equal to federal credit for state death taxes less any amounts paid on state inheritance tax. Maximum total state inheritance and state estate tax is equal to the maximum allowable federal estate tax credit for state death taxes.

MASSACHUSETTS

State Law Description: Massachusetts General Laws; Chapter 191, Sections 1+.
Court With Probate Jurisdiction: Probate and Family Court.
Minimum Age for Disposing of Property by Will: 18.
Required Number of Witnesses: Two. (Three recommended.)
May Witnesses Be Beneficiaries?: No.
Are There Provisions for Self-Proving Wills?: Yes. (Use the Affidavit in Chapter 13.)
Are Living Wills Recognized?: Not by statute. However, you may still draft a living will, contact *Choice in Dying* or refer to Appendix VII.
How Does Divorce Affect the Will?: Revokes the will as to the divorced spouse.
How Does Marriage Affect the Will?: Revokes the will.
Who Must Be Mentioned in the Will?: Children, born or adopted; grandchildren (if of deceased child); surviving spouse.
Spouse's Right to Property Regardless of Will: Generally, the surviving spouse is entitled to 1/2 of the deceased spouse's estate if there are no children, and only 1/3 if there are children. However, please refer directly to the statute as the provisions are detailed.
Laws of Intestate Distribution (Distribution If Decedent Leaves No Will):
Spouse and Children of Spouse Surviving: 1/2 to spouse and 1/2 to children equally or grandchildren per stirpes.
Spouse and Children Not of Spouse Surviving: 1/2 to spouse and 1/2 to children equally or grandchildren per stirpes.
Spouse, but No Children or Parent(s) Surviving: $200,000 and 1/2 of balance to spouse and 1/2 of balance to brothers and sisters equally or their children per stirpes; or if none, to next of kin; or if none, all to spouse.
Spouse and Parent(s), but No Children Surviving: $200,000 and 1/2 of balance to spouse and 1/2 of balance to parents equally or the surviving parent.
Children, but No Spouse Surviving: All to children equally or to their children per stirpes.
Parent(s), but No Spouse or Children Surviving: All to parents equally, or to the surviving parent.
No Spouse, Children or Parent(s) Surviving: All to brothers and sisters equally or their children per stirpes; or if none, to the next of kin.
Forms of Property Ownership: Common law state. Tenancy in common, joint tenancy and tenancy by entirety recognized. Joint ownership by husband and wife creates tenancy in common, unless otherwise stated.
State Restrictions on Gifts to Charities?: No.
State Gift, Inheritance or Estate Taxes: No gift tax; no inheritance tax; imposes state estate tax of up to 16% (not tied to federal estate tax credit).
Note: Fill-in-the-blank statutory will forms available from probate court and legal stationery stores.

MICHIGAN

State Law Description: Michigan Compiled Laws Annotated; Sections 600.801+, 700.121+.

Court With Probate Jurisdiction: Probate Court.

Minimum Age for Disposing of Property by Will: 18.

Required Number of Witnesses: Two. (Three recommended.)

May Witnesses Be Beneficiaries?: No.

Are There Provisions for Self-Proving Wills?: Yes. (Use the Affidavit in Chapter 13.)

Are Living Wills Recognized?: Not by statute. However, you may still draft a living will, contact *Choice in Dying* or refer to Appendix VII.

How Does Divorce Affect the Will?: Revokes will as to divorced spouse.

How Does Marriage Affect the Will?: Revokes the will as to the spouse if she or he is not otherwise provided for. Spouse may still be entitled to her or his statutory share under the state intestate laws.

Who Must Be Mentioned in the Will?: Children, born or adopted; surviving spouse.

Spouse's Right to Property Regardless of Will: Generally, the surviving spouse is entitled to 1/2 of the deceased spouse's estate if there are no children, and only 1/3 if there are children. However, please refer directly to the statute as the provisions are detailed.

Laws of Intestate Distribution (Distribution If Decedent Leaves No Will):

    Spouse and Children of Spouse Surviving: $60,000 and 1/2 of balance to spouse and 1/2 of balance to children per stirpes.

    Spouse and Children Not of Spouse Surviving: 1/2 to spouse and 1/2 to children per stirpes.

    Spouse, but No Children or Parent(s) Surviving: All to spouse.

    Spouse and Parent(s), but No Children Surviving: $60,000 and 1/2 of balance to spouse and 1/2 of balance to parents or surviving parent.

    Children, but No Spouse Surviving: All to children or to their children per stirpes.

    Parent(s), but No Spouse or Children Surviving: All to parents equally, or to the surviving parent.

    No Spouse, Children or Parent(s) Surviving: All to brothers and sisters equally or to their children per stirpes; or if none, 1/2 to maternal grandparents or their children per stirpes and 1/2 to paternal grandparents or their children per stirpes.

Forms of Property Ownership: Common law state. Tenancy in common, joint tenancy, tenancy by entirety recognized. Joint tenancy created only if stated. Joint tenancy by spouses and joint ownership of real estate by spouses presumed tenancy by entirety unless otherwise stated. Joint tenancy with right of survivorship recognized for bank accounts, securities, safe deposit box contents; intent must be in writing.

State Restrictions on Gifts to Charities?: No.

State Gift, Inheritance or Estate Taxes: No gift tax; imposes an inheritance tax of up to 17%; imposes state estate tax equal to federal credit for state death taxes less any amounts paid on state inheritance tax. Maximum total state inheritance and state estate tax is equal to the maximum allowable federal estate tax credit for state death taxes.
Note: Fill-in-the-blank statutory will forms available from probate court and legal stationery stores.

MINNESOTA

State Law Description: Minnesota Statutes Annotated; Chapters 524.1-101+.

Court With Probate Jurisdiction: Probate Court.

Minimum Age for Disposing of Property by Will: 18.

Required Number of Witnesses: Two. (Three recommended.)

May Witnesses Be Beneficiaries?: Yes. (Not recommended.)

Are There Provisions for Self-Proving Wills?: Yes. (Use the Affidavit in Chapter 13.)

Are Living Wills Recognized?: Yes, under the "Minnesota Adult Health Care Decisions Act."

How Does Divorce Affect the Will?: Revokes the will as to the divorced spouse.

How Does Marriage Affect the Will?: Revokes the will as to the spouse if she or he is not otherwise provided for. Spouse may still be entitled to her or his statutory share under the state intestate laws.

Who Must Be Mentioned in the Will?: Children, born or adopted; grandchildren (if of deceased child); surviving spouse.

Spouse's Right to Property Regardless of Will: Generally, the surviving spouse is entitled to 1/2 of the deceased spouse's estate if there are no children, and only 1/3 if there are children. However, please refer directly to the statute as the provisions are detailed.

Laws of Intestate Distribution (Distribution If Decedent Leaves No Will):

Spouse and Children of Spouse Surviving: $70,000 and 1/2 of balance to spouse and 1/2 of balance to children or grandchildren per stirpes.

Spouse and Children Not of Spouse Surviving: 1/2 to spouse and 1/2 to children or grandchildren per stirpes.

Spouse, but No Children or Parent(s) Surviving: All to spouse.

Spouse and Parent(s), but No Children Surviving: All to spouse.

Children, but No Spouse Surviving: All to children equally or to their children per stirpes.

Parent(s), but No Spouse or Children Surviving: All to parents equally, or to the surviving parent.

No Spouse, Children or Parent(s) Surviving: All to brothers and sisters equally or their children per stirpes; or if none, to the next of kin.

Forms of Property Ownership: Common law state. Tenancy in common presumed unless joint tenancy in writing. No tenancy by entirety.

State Restrictions on Gifts to Charities?: No.

State Gift, Inheritance or Estate Taxes: No gift tax; no inheritance tax; imposes state estate tax equal to federal credit for state death taxes.

MISSISSIPPI

State Law Description: Mississippi Code Annotated; Section 91, Chapters 1-1+.
Court With Probate Jurisdiction: Chancery Court.
Minimum Age for Disposing of Property by Will: 18.
Required Number of Witnesses: Two. (Three recommended.)
May Witnesses Be Beneficiaries?: No.
Are There Provisions for Self-Proving Wills?: Yes. (Use the Affidavit in Chapter 13.)
Are Living Wills Recognized?: Yes, under the "Mississippi Withdrawal of Life-Saving Mechanisms Act."
How Does Divorce Affect the Will?: Does not revoke the will.
How Does Marriage Affect the Will?: Does not revoke the will.
Who Must Be Mentioned in the Will?: Children, born or adopted; surviving spouse.
Spouse's Right to Property Regardless of Will: Generally, the surviving spouse is entitled to 1/2 of the deceased spouse's estate if there are no children, and only 1/3 if there are children. However, please refer directly to the statute as the provisions are detailed.
Laws of Intestate Distribution (Distribution If Decedent Leaves No Will):
   Spouse and Children of Spouse Surviving: Spouse and any surviving children or grandchildren each take equal shares.
   Spouse and Children Not of Spouse Surviving: Spouse and any surviving children or grandchildren each take equal shares.
   Spouse, but No Children or Parent(s) Surviving: All to spouse.
   Spouse and Parent(s), but No Children Surviving: All to spouse.
   Children, but No Spouse Surviving: All to children equally or to their children per stirpes.
   Parent(s), but No Spouse or Children Surviving: All to parents, brothers, and sisters equally, or to children of brothers and sisters per stirpes. If no brothers or sisters or children of brothers or sisters, all to parents equally or the surviving parent.
   No Spouse, Children or Parent(s) Surviving: All to brothers and sisters equally, or to their children per stirpes; or if none, to grandparents, uncles, and aunts equally, or to their children per stirpes; or if none, to the next of kin.
Forms of Property Ownership: Common law state. Tenancy in common, joint tenancy and tenancy by entirety recognized. Ownership by two or more persons presumes tenancy in common unless joint tenancy stated.
State Restrictions on Gifts to Charities?: Yes. If extensive gifts to charities are contemplated, please refer directly to statute or consult an attorney.
State Gift, Inheritance or Estate Taxes: No gift tax; no inheritance tax; imposes state estate tax of up to 16%. (State estate tax not tied to federal credit for state death taxes.)

MISSOURI

State Law Description: Missouri Annotated Statutes; Sections 472.005+, 474.310+.
Court With Probate Jurisdiction: Circuit Court.
Minimum Age for Disposing of Property by Will: 18.
Required Number of Witnesses: Two. (Three recommended.)
May Witnesses Be Beneficiaries?: No.
Are There Provisions for Self-Proving Wills?: Yes. (Use the Affidavit in Chapter 13.)
Are Living Wills Recognized?: Yes, under the "Missouri Life Support Declaration Act."
How Does Divorce Affect the Will?: Revokes the will as to the divorced spouse.
How Does Marriage Affect the Will?: Revokes the will as to the spouse if she or he is not otherwise provided for. Spouse may still be entitled to her or his statutory share under the state intestate laws.
Who Must Be Mentioned in the Will?: Children, born or adopted; surviving spouse.
Spouse's Right to Property Regardless of Will: Generally, the surviving spouse is entitled to 1/2 of the deceased spouse's estate if there are no children, and only 1/3 if there are children. However, please refer directly to the statute as the provisions are detailed.
Laws of Intestate Distribution (Distribution If Decedent Leaves No Will):
  Spouse and Children of Spouse Surviving: $20,000 and 1/2 of balance to spouse and 1/2 of balance to children or grandchildren per stirpes.
  Spouse and Children Not of Spouse Surviving: 1/2 to spouse and 1/2 to children or grandchildren per stirpes.
  Spouse, but No Children or Parent(s) Surviving: All to spouse.
  Spouse and Parent(s), but No Children Surviving: $20,000 and 1/2 of balance to spouse and 1/2 of balance to parents or surviving parent.
  Children, but No Spouse Surviving: All to children equally or to their children per stirpes.
  Parent(s), but No Spouse or Children Surviving: All to parents, brothers, and sisters equally, or to their children per stirpes; or if none, all to parents or to the surviving parent.
  No Spouse, Children or Parent(s) Surviving: All to brothers and sisters equally or to their children per stirpes; or if none, to grandparents, uncles, and aunts and their children per stirpes; or if none, to the nearest lineal ancestor and their children.
Forms of Property Ownership: Common law state. Tenancy in common, joint tenancy and tenancy by entirety recognized. Ownership by two or more persons presumes tenancy in common unless joint tenancy stated.
State Restrictions on Gifts to Charities?: No.
State Gift, Inheritance or Estate Taxes: No gift tax; no inheritance tax; imposes state estate tax equal to federal credit for state death taxes.

MONTANA

State Law Description: Montana Code Annotated; Sections 72, Titles 1-101+.

Court With Probate Jurisdiction: District Court.

Minimum Age for Disposing of Property by Will: 18.

Required Number of Witnesses: Two. (Three recommended.)

May Witnesses Be Beneficiaries?: No.

Are There Provisions for Self-Proving Wills?: Yes. (Use the Affidavit in Chapter 13.)

Are Living Wills Recognized?: Yes, under the "Montana Rights of the Terminally Ill Act."

How Does Divorce Affect the Will?: Revokes the will as to the divorced spouse.

How Does Marriage Affect the Will?: Revokes the will as to the spouse if she or he is not otherwise provided for. Spouse may still be entitled to her or his statutory share under the state intestate laws.

Who Must Be Mentioned in the Will?: Children, born or adopted; surviving spouse.

Spouse's Right to Property Regardless of Will: The surviving spouse is entitled to 1/3 of the "augmented" estate of the deceased spouse. In general, the "augmented" estate includes both the property that passes under the will and any other property that passes by other "non-will" transfers, such as under the terms of a living trust or a joint tenancy arrangement.

Laws of Intestate Distribution (Distribution If Decedent Leaves No Will):

Spouse and Children of Spouse Surviving: All to spouse.

Spouse and Children Not of Spouse Surviving: If one child surviving, 1/2 to spouse and 1/2 to child; if more than 1 child surviving, 1/3 to spouse and 2/3 to children equally.

Spouse, but No Children or Parent(s) Surviving: All to spouse.

Spouse and Parent(s), but No Children Surviving: All to spouse.

Children, but No Spouse Surviving: All to children equally or to their children per stirpes.

Parent(s), but No Spouse or Children Surviving: All to parents equally, or to the surviving parent.

No Spouse, Children or Parent(s) Surviving: All to brothers and sisters equally or their children per stirpes; or if none, 1/2 to paternal and 1/2 to maternal grandparents or their children per stirpes.

Forms of Property Ownership: Common law state. Partnership interests, tenancy in common and joint tenancy (called "interests in common" and "joint interests") recognized. No tenancy by entirety in personal property. Tenancy in common presumed unless joint tenancy stated.

State Restrictions on Gifts to Charities?: Yes. If extensive gifts to charities are contemplated, please refer directly to statute or consult an attorney.

State Gift, Inheritance or Estate Taxes: No gift tax; imposes an inheritance tax of up to 32%; imposes state estate tax equal to federal credit for state death taxes less any amounts paid on state inheritance tax. Maximum total state inheritance and state estate tax is equal to the maximum allowable federal estate tax credit for state death taxes.

NEBRASKA

State Law Description: Revised Statutes of Nebraska; Chapter 30, Sections 2201+,2326+.

Court With Probate Jurisdiction: County Court.

Minimum Age for Disposing of Property by Will: 18.

Required Number of Witnesses: Two. (Three recommended.)

May Witnesses Be Beneficiaries?: Yes. (Not recommended.)

Are There Provisions for Self-Proving Wills?: Yes. (Use the Affidavit in Chapter 13.)

Are Living Wills Recognized?: Yes, under the "Nebraska Rights of the Terminally Ill Act."

How Does Divorce Affect the Will?: Revokes the will as to the divorced spouse.

How Does Marriage Affect the Will?: Revokes the will as to the spouse if she or he is not otherwise provided for. Spouse may still be entitled to her or his statutory share under the state intestate laws.

Who Must Be Mentioned in the Will?: Children, born or adopted; surviving spouse.

Spouse's Right to Property Regardless of Will: The surviving spouse is entitled to 1/3 of the "augmented" estate of the deceased spouse. In general, the "augmented" estate includes both the property that passes under the will and any other property that passes by other "non-will" transfers, such as under the terms of a living trust or a joint tenancy arrangement.

Laws of Intestate Distribution (Distribution If Decedent Leaves No Will):

  Spouse and Children of Spouse Surviving: $50,000 and 1/2 of balance to spouse and 1/2 of balance to children.

  Spouse and Children Not of Spouse Surviving: 1/2 to spouse and 1/2 to children.

  Spouse, but No Children or Parent(s) Surviving: All to spouse.

  Spouse and Parent(s), but No Children Surviving: $50,000 and 1/2 of balance to spouse and 1/2 of balance to parents or surviving parent.

  Children, but No Spouse Surviving: All to children equally or to their children per stirpes.

  Parent(s), but No Spouse or Children Surviving: All to parents equally, or to the surviving parent.

  No Spouse, Children or Parent(s) Surviving: All to brothers and sisters equally, or their children per stirpes; or if none, 1/2 to paternal and 1/2 to maternal grandparents or their children per stirpes.

Forms of Property Ownership: Common law state. Partnership interests, tenancy in common and joint tenancy (called "interests in common" and "joint interests") recognized. No tenancy by entirety in personal property. Tenancy in common presumed unless joint tenancy stated.

State Restrictions on Gifts to Charities?: No.

State Gift, Inheritance or Estate Taxes: No gift tax; imposes an inheritance tax of up to 18%; imposes state estate tax equal to federal credit for state death taxes less any amounts paid on state inheritance tax. Maximum total state inheritance and state estate tax is equal to the maximum allowable federal estate tax credit for state death taxes.

NEVADA

State Law Description: Nevada Revised Statutes Annotated; Chapters 133.000-150.999.
Court With Probate Jurisdiction: District Court.
Minimum Age for Disposing of Property by Will: 18.
Required Number of Witnesses: Two. (Three recommended.)
May Witnesses Be Beneficiaries?: No.
Are There Provisions for Self-Proving Wills?: Yes. (Use the Affidavit in Chapter 13.)
Are Living Wills Recognized?: Yes, under the "Nevada Uniform Act on the Rights of the Terminally Ill."
How Does Divorce Affect the Will?: Revokes the will as to the divorced spouse.
How Does Marriage Affect the Will?: Revokes the will as to the spouse if she or he is not otherwise provided for. Spouse may still be entitled to her or his statutory share under the state intestate laws.
Who Must Be Mentioned in the Will?: Statute contains detailed provisions regarding this. Please refer directly to statute or consult an attorney if this is a critical factor.
Spouse's Right to Property Regardless of Will: Community property right to 1/2 of the deceased spouse's "community" property.
Laws of Intestate Distribution (Distribution If Decedent Leaves No Will):
> ***Spouse and Children of Spouse Surviving:*** All of decedent's community property to spouse. If only 1 child is surviving, 1/2 of decedent's separate property to spouse and 1/2 to child or grandchildren per stirpes; if more than 1 child is surviving, 1/3 of separate property to spouse and 2/3 to the children or grandchildren per stirpes.
> ***Spouse and Children Not of Spouse Surviving:*** Same as above for "Spouse and Children of Spouse Surviving."
> ***Spouse, but No Children or Parent(s) Surviving:*** All of decedent's community property to spouse. 1/2 of decedent's separate property to spouse and 1/2 to brothers and sisters equally or their children per stirpes; or if none, all to spouse.
> ***Spouse and Parent(s), but No Children Surviving:*** All of decedent's community property to spouse. 1/2 of decedent's separate property to spouse and 1/2 to parents or surviving parent.
> ***Children, but No Spouse Surviving:*** All to children or to their children per stirpes.
> ***Parent(s), but No Spouse or Children Surviving:*** All to parents equally, or to the surviving parent.
> ***No Spouse, Children or Parent(s) Surviving:*** All to brothers and sisters equally, or their children per stirpes; or if none, to the next of kin.

Forms of Property Ownership: Community property state. Tenancy in common, joint tenancy and community property recognized. No tenancy by entirety.
State Restrictions on Gifts to Charities?: No.
State Gift, Inheritance or Estate Taxes: No gift tax; no inheritance tax; no state estate tax.

NEW HAMPSHIRE

State Law Description: New Hampshire Revised Statutes; Chapters 547:1+, 551:1+.
Court With Probate Jurisdiction: Probate Court.
Minimum Age for Disposing of Property by Will: 18, or married (any age).
Required Number of Witnesses: Three.
May Witnesses Be Beneficiaries?: No.
Are There Provisions for Self-Proving Wills?: Yes. (A locally drafted self-proving affidavit is advised.)
Are Living Wills Recognized?: Yes, under the "New Hampshire Living Wills Act."
How Does Divorce Affect the Will?: Does not revoke the will.
How Does Marriage Affect the Will?: Revokes the will if a child is later born to the marriage.
Who Must Be Mentioned in the Will?: Children, born or adopted; grandchildren; surviving spouse.
Spouse's Right to Property Regardless of Will: Generally, the surviving spouse is entitled to 1/2 of the deceased spouse's estate if there are no children, and only 1/3 if there are children. However, please refer directly to the statute as the provisions are detailed.
Laws of Intestate Distribution (Distribution If Decedent Leaves No Will):
   Spouse and Children of Spouse Surviving: $50,000 and 1/2 of balance to spouse and 1/2 of balance to children or grandchildren per stirpes.
   Spouse and Children Not of Spouse Surviving: 1/2 to spouse and 1/2 to children or grandchildren per stirpes.
   Spouse, but No Children or Parent(s) Surviving: All to spouse.
   Spouse and Parent(s), but No Children Surviving: $50,000 and 1/2 of balance to spouse and 1/2 of balance to parents or surviving parent.
   Children, but No Spouse Surviving: All to children or to their children per stirpes.
   Parent(s), but No Spouse or Children Surviving: All to parents equally, or to the surviving parent.
   No Spouse, Children or Parent(s) Surviving: All to brothers and sisters equally, or their children per stirpes; or if none, 1/2 to maternal and 1/2 to paternal grandparents or their children per stirpes.
Forms of Property Ownership: Common law state. Tenancy in common presumed unless joint tenancy stated. Ownership by spouses creates joint tenancy. No tenancy by entirety.
State Restrictions on Gifts to Charities?: No.
State Gift, Inheritance or Estate Taxes: No gift tax; imposes an inheritance tax of up to 15%; imposes state estate tax equal to federal credit for state death taxes less any amounts paid on state inheritance tax. Maximum total state inheritance and state estate tax is equal to the maximum allowable federal estate tax credit for state death taxes.

NEW JERSEY

State Law Description: New Jersey Revised Statutes; Title 3B: Chapters 3-1+.
Court With Probate Jurisdiction: Surrogate's Court.
Minimum Age for Disposing of Property by Will: 21.
Required Number of Witnesses: Two. (Three recommended.)
May Witnesses Be Beneficiaries?: Yes. (Not recommended.)
Are There Provisions for Self-Proving Wills?: Yes. (Use the Affidavit in Chapter 13.)
Are Living Wills Recognized?: Yes, under the "New Jersey Advance Directives for Health Care Act."
How Does Divorce Affect the Will?: Revokes the will as to the divorced spouse.
How Does Marriage Affect the Will?: Revokes the will as to the spouse if she or he is not otherwise provided for. Spouse may still be entitled to her or his statutory share under the state intestate laws.
Who Must Be Mentioned in the Will?: Children, born or adopted; grandchildren; surviving spouse.
Spouse's Right to Property Regardless of Will: The surviving spouse is entitled to 1/3 of the "augmented" estate of the deceased spouse. In general, the "augmented" estate includes both the property that passes under the will and any other property that passes by other "non-will" transfers, such as under the terms of a living trust or a joint tenancy arrangement.
Laws of Intestate Distribution (Distribution If Decedent Leaves No Will):
   Spouse and Children of Spouse Surviving: $50,000 and 1/2 of balance to spouse and 1/2 of balance to children or grandchildren per stirpes.
   Spouse and Children Not of Spouse Surviving: 1/2 to spouse and 1/2 to children or grandchildren per stirpes.
   Spouse, but No Children or Parent(s) Surviving: All to spouse.
   Spouse and Parent(s), but No Children Surviving: $50,000 and 1/2 of balance to spouse and 1/2 of balance to parents or surviving parent.
   Children, but No Spouse Surviving: All to children or to their children per stirpes.
   Parent(s), but No Spouse or Children Surviving: All to parents equally, or to the surviving parent.
   No Spouse, Children or Parent(s) Surviving: All to brothers and sisters equally, or their children per stirpes; or if none, 1/2 to maternal and 1/2 to paternal grandparents or their children per stirpes.
Forms of Property Ownership: Common law state. Tenancy in common, joint tenancy and tenancy by entirety recognized. Ownership by spouses presumes tenancy by entirety unless stated otherwise. Tenancy in common presumed unless joint tenancy stated.
State Restrictions on Gifts to Charities?: No.

State Gift, Inheritance or Estate Taxes: No gift tax; imposes an inheritance tax of up to 16%; imposes state estate tax equal to federal credit for state death taxes less any amounts paid on state inheritance tax. Maximum total state inheritance and state estate tax is equal to the maximum allowable federal estate tax credit for state death taxes.

NEW MEXICO

State Law Description: New Mexico Statutes Annotated; Sections 45-2-101+.
Court With Probate Jurisdiction: Probate or District Court.
Minimum Age for Disposing of Property by Will: 18.
Required Number of Witnesses: Two. (Three recommended.)
May Witnesses Be Beneficiaries?: Yes. (Not recommended.)
Are There Provisions for Self-Proving Wills?: Yes. (Use the Affidavit in Chapter 13.)
Are Living Wills Recognized?: Yes, under the "New Mexico Right to Die Act."
How Does Divorce Affect the Will?: Revokes the will as to the divorced spouse.
How Does Marriage Affect the Will?: Revokes the will as to the spouse if she or he is not otherwise provided for. Spouse may still be entitled to her or his statutory share under the state intestate laws.
Who Must Be Mentioned in the Will?: Children, born or adopted; surviving spouse.
Spouse's Right to Property Regardless of Will: Community property right to 1/2 of the deceased spouse's "community" property.
Laws of Intestate Distribution (Distribution If Decedent Leaves No Will):
  Spouse and Children of Spouse Surviving: All of decedent's community property to spouse. 1/4 of decedent's separate property to spouse and 3/4 to children or grandchildren per stirpes.
  Spouse and Children Not of Spouse Surviving: All of decedent's community property to spouse. 1/4 of decedent's separate property to spouse and 3/4 to children or grandchildren per stirpes.
  Spouse, but No Children or Parent(s) Surviving: All to spouse.
  Spouse and Parent(s), but No Children Surviving: All to spouse.
  Children, but No Spouse Surviving: All to children equally or to their children per stirpes.
  Parent(s), but No Spouse or Children Surviving: All to parents equally, or to the surviving parent.
  No Spouse, Children or Parent(s) Surviving: All to brothers and sisters equally, or their children per stirpes; or if none, 1/2 to maternal and 1/2 to paternal grandparents or their children per stirpes.
Forms of Property Ownership: Community property state. Tenancy in common, joint tenancy, community property recognized. Spouses may hold real estate as joint tenants. No tenancy by entirety.
State Restrictions on Gifts to Charities?: No.
State Gift, Inheritance or Estate Taxes: No gift tax; no inheritance tax; imposes state estate tax equal to federal credit for state death taxes.

NEW YORK

State Law Description: New York Consolidated Laws; Estates, Powers, and Trusts.

Court With Probate Jurisdiction: Surrogate's Court.

Minimum Age for Disposing of Property by Will: 18.

Required Number of Witnesses: Two. (Three recommended.)

May Witnesses Be Beneficiaries?: No.

Are There Provisions for Self-Proving Wills?: Yes. (Use the Affidavit in Chapter 13).

Are Living Wills Recognized?: Not by statute. However, you may still draft a living will, contact *Choice in Dying*, or refer to Appendix VII.

How Does Divorce Affect the Will?: Revokes the will as to the divorced spouse.

How Does Marriage Affect the Will?: Does not revoke the will.

Who Must Be Mentioned in the Will?: Children, born or adopted; surviving spouse.

Spouse's Right to Property Regardless of Will: Generally, the surviving spouse is entitled to 1/2 of the deceased spouse's estate if there are no children, and only 1/3 if there are children. However, please refer directly to the statute as the provisions are detailed.

Laws of Intestate Distribution (Distribution If Decedent Leaves No Will):

Spouse and Children of Spouse Surviving: If only 1 child or grandchild surviving, $4,000 and 1/2 of balance to spouse and 1/2 of balance to child or grandchild. If more than 1 child or grandchild, $4,000 and 1/3 of balance to spouse and 2/3 of balance to children or grandchildren per stirpes.

Spouse and Children Not of Spouse Surviving: Same as above for "Spouse and Children of Spouse Surviving."

Spouse, but No Children or Parent(s) Surviving: All to spouse.

Spouse and Parent(s), but No Children Surviving: $25,000 and 1/2 of balance to spouse and 1/2 of balance to parents or surviving parent.

Children, but No Spouse Surviving: All to children equally or to their children per stirpes.

Parent(s), but No Spouse or Children Surviving: All to parents equally, or to the surviving parent.

No Spouse, Children or Parent(s) Surviving: All to brothers and sisters equally, or their children per stirpes; or if none, to grandparents equally or their children per capita; or if none, to the next of kin.

Forms of Property Ownership: Common law state. Tenancy in common, joint tenancy and tenancy by entirety recognized. Joint ownership by spouses presumes tenancy by entirety unless specified otherwise. Joint ownership by couples not legally married but who are described as husband and wife presumes joint tenancy unless tenancy in common stated. Tenancy in common presumed unless joint tenancy stated. Tenancy by entirety in personal property not recognized.

State Restrictions on Gifts to Charities?: No.

State Gift, Inheritance or Estate Taxes: Imposes a gift tax; no inheritance tax; imposes a state estate tax of up to 21% or not less than any federal credit for state death taxes.

NORTH CAROLINA

State Law Description: North Carolina General Statutes; Chapters 28A-1+,31-1+, 47-1+.

Court With Probate Jurisdiction: Superior Court.

Minimum Age for Disposing of Property by Will: 18.

Required Number of Witnesses: Two. (Three recommended.)

May Witnesses Be Beneficiaries?: No.

Are There Provisions for Self-Proving Wills?: Yes. (Use the Affidavit in Chapter 13.)

Are Living Wills Recognized?: Yes, under the "North Carolina Right to Natural Death Act."

How Does Divorce Affect the Will?: Revokes the will as to the divorced spouse.

How Does Marriage Affect the Will?: Does not revoke the will.

Who Must Be Mentioned in the Will?: Children, born or adopted; surviving spouse.

Spouse's Right to Property Regardless of Will: Generally, the surviving spouse is entitled to 1/2 of the deceased spouse's estate if there are no children, and only 1/3 if there are children. Please refer directly to the statute for details.

Laws of Intestate Distribution (Distribution If Decedent Leaves No Will):

Spouse and Children of Spouse Surviving: If only 1 child surviving, $15,000 (from any personal property, if any) and 1/2 of balance to spouse and 1/2 of balance to children or grandchildren per stirpes. If more than one child, $15,000 (from any personal property, if any) and 1/3 of balance to spouse and 2/3 of balance to children or grandchildren per stirpes.

Spouse and Children Not of Spouse Surviving: Same as above for "Spouse and Children of Spouse Surviving."

Spouse, but No Children or Parent(s) Surviving: All to spouse.

Spouse and Parent(s), but No Children Surviving: $25,000 (from personal property, if any) and 1/2 of balance to spouse and 1/2 of balance to parents or surviving parent.

Children, but No Spouse Surviving: All to children equally or to their children per stirpes.

Parent(s), but No Spouse or Children Surviving: All to parents equally, or to the surviving parent.

No Spouse, Children or Parent(s) Surviving: All to brothers and sisters equally, or their children per stirpes; or if none, 1/2 to maternal and 1/2 to paternal grandparents or their children per stirpes.

Forms of Property Ownership: Common law state. Tenancy in common, joint tenancy and tenancy by entirety recognized. Tenancy by entirety in personal property not recognized.

State Restrictions on Gifts to Charities?: No.

State Gift, Inheritance or Estate Taxes: Imposes a gift tax;
imposes an inheritance tax of up to 17%; imposes a state estate tax
equal to federal credit for state death taxes less any amounts paid on
state inheritance tax. Maximum total state inheritance and state estate tax
is equal to the maximum allowable federal estate tax credit for state death
taxes.

NORTH DAKOTA

State Law Description: North Dakota Century Code; Chapters 30.1-01+.
Court With Probate Jurisdiction: County Court.
Minimum Age for Disposing of Property by Will: 18.
Required Number of Witnesses: Two. (Three recommended.)
May Witnesses Be Beneficiaries?: Yes. (Not recommended.)
Are There Provisions for Self-Proving Wills?: Yes. (Use the Affidavit in Chapter 13.)
Are Living Wills Recognized?: Yes, under the "North Dakota Uniform Rights of the Terminally Ill Act."
How Does Divorce Affect the Will?: Revokes the will as to the divorced spouse.
How Does Marriage Affect the Will?: Revokes the will as to the spouse if she or he is not otherwise provided for. Spouse may still be entitled to her or his statutory share under the state intestate laws.
Who Must Be Mentioned in the Will?: Children, born or adopted; surviving spouse.
Spouse's Right to Property Regardless of Will: The surviving spouse is entitled to 1/3 of the "augmented" estate of the deceased spouse. In general, the "augmented" estate includes both the property that passes under the will and any other property that passes by other "non-will" transfers, such as under the terms of a living trust or a joint tenancy arrangement.
Laws of Intestate Distribution (Distribution If Decedent Leaves No Will):
  Spouse and Children of Spouse Surviving: $50,000 and 1/2 of balance to spouse and 1/2 of balance to children or grandchildren per stirpes.
  Spouse and Children Not of Spouse Surviving: 1/2 to spouse and 1/2 to children or grandchildren per stirpes.
  Spouse, but No Children or Parent(s) Surviving: All to spouse.
  Spouse and Parent(s), but No Children Surviving: $50,000 and 1/2 of balance to spouse and 1/2 of balance to parents or surviving parent.
  Children, but No Spouse Surviving: All to children equally or to their children per stirpes.
  Parent(s), but No Spouse or Children Surviving: All to parents equally, or to the surviving parent.
  No Spouse, Children or Parent(s) Surviving: All to brothers and sisters equally, or their children per stirpes; or if none, 1/2 to maternal and 1/2 to paternal next of kin.
Forms of Property Ownership: Common law state. Tenancy in common and joint tenancy recognized. No tenancy by entirety.
State Restrictions on Gifts to Charities?: No.
State Gift, Inheritance or Estate Taxes: No gift tax; no inheritance tax; imposes state estate tax equal to federal credit for state death taxes.

OHIO

State Law Description: Ohio Revised Code Annotated; Sections 2101.01+, 2107.01+.
Court With Probate Jurisdiction: Court of Common Pleas.
Minimum Age for Disposing of Property by Will: 18.
Required Number of Witnesses: Two. (Three recommended.)
May Witnesses Be Beneficiaries?: No.
Are There Provisions for Self-Proving Wills?: Not in statutes. However self-proving affidavits have been accepted in the courts. (Use the Affidavit in Chapter 13.)
Are Living Wills Recognized?: Yes, under "Ohio Modified Uniform Rights of the Terminally Ill Act."
How Does Divorce Affect the Will?: Revokes the will as to the divorced spouse.
How Does Marriage Affect the Will?: Does not revoke the will.
Who Must Be Mentioned in the Will?: Children, born or adopted; surviving spouse.
Spouse's Right to Property Regardless of Will: Generally, the surviving spouse is entitled to 1/2 of the deceased spouse's estate if there are no children, and only 1/3 if there are children. However, please refer directly to the statute as the provisions are detailed.
Laws of Intestate Distribution (Distribution If Decedent Leaves No Will):
  Spouse and Children of Spouse Surviving: If only one child surviving, $30,000 and 1/2 of balance to spouse and 1/2 of balance to children or grandchildren per stirpes. If more than one child surviving, $30,000 and 1/3 of balance to spouse and 2/3 of balance to children or grandchildren per stirpes.
  Spouse and Children Not of Spouse Surviving: If only one child surviving, $10,000 and 1/2 of balance to spouse and 1/2 of balance to children or grandchildren per stirpes. If more than one child surviving, $10,000 and 1/3 of balance to spouse and 2/3 of balance to children or grandchildren per stirpes.
  Spouse, but No Children or Parent(s) Surviving: All to spouse.
  Spouse and Parent(s), but No Children Surviving: All to spouse.
  Children, but No Spouse Surviving: All to children or to their children per stirpes.
  Parent(s), but No Spouse or Children Surviving: All to parents equally, or to the surviving parent.
  No Spouse, Children or Parent(s) Surviving: All to brothers and sisters equally, or their children per stirpes; or if none, 1/2 to maternal and 1/2 to paternal grandparents or their children per stirpes; or if none, to the next of kin.
Forms of Property Ownership: Common law state. Tenancy in common, joint tenancy and tenancy by entirety recognized. If joint tenancy, must be stated.
State Restrictions on Gifts to Charities?: Yes. If extensive gifts to charities are contemplated, please refer directly to statute or consult an attorney.

State Gift, Inheritance or Estate Taxes: No gift tax; no inheritance tax; imposes a state estate tax of up to 7% or not less than any federal credit for state death taxes.

OKLAHOMA

State Law Description: Oklahoma Statutes Annotated; Title 58, Section 1+, Title 84, Sections 1+.

Court With Probate Jurisdiction: District Court.

Minimum Age for Disposing of Property by Will: 18.

Required Number of Witnesses: Two. (Three recommended.)

May Witnesses Be Beneficiaries?: Yes. (Not recommended.)

Are There Provisions for Self-Proving Wills?: Yes. (Use the Affidavit in Chapter 13.)

Are Living Wills Recognized?: Yes, under the "Oklahoma Natural Death Act."

How Does Divorce Affect the Will?: Revokes the will as to the divorced spouse.

How Does Marriage Affect the Will?: Revokes the will if a child is later born into the marriage.

Who Must Be Mentioned in the Will?: Children, born or adopted; surviving spouse.

Spouse's Right to Property Regardless of Will: Generally, the surviving spouse is entitled to 1/2 of the deceased spouse's estate if there are no children, and only 1/3 if there are children. However, please refer to the statute for details.

Laws of Intestate Distribution (Distribution If Decedent Leaves No Will):

Spouse and Children of Spouse Surviving: 1/2 to spouse and 1/2 to children or grandchildren per stirpes.

Spouse and Children Not of Spouse Surviving: 1/2 of property acquired during the marriage by joint effort to spouse, and balance to children and spouse in equal shares.

Spouse, but No Children or Parent(s) Surviving: All property acquired during the marriage by joint effort to spouse. 1/3 of other property to spouse and 1/3 to maternal and 1/3 to paternal grandparents or their children per stirpes; or if none, to the next of kin.

Spouse and Parent(s), but No Children Surviving: All property acquired during the marriage by joint effort to spouse. 1/3 of other property to spouse and 2/3 to parents or surviving parent per stirpes.

Children, but No Spouse Surviving: All to children equally or grandchildren per stirpes.

Parent(s), but No Spouse or Children Surviving: All to parents equally, or to the surviving parent.

No Spouse, Children or Parent(s) Surviving: All to brothers and sisters equally, or their children per stirpes; or if none, 1/2 to maternal and 1/2 to paternal grandparents or their children per stirpes; or if none, to the next of kin.

Forms of Property Ownership: Common law state. Tenancy in common, joint tenancy and tenancy by entirety recognized. Rights of survivorship must be stated.

State Restrictions on Gifts to Charities?: No.

State Gift, Inheritance or Estate Taxes: No gift tax; no inheritance tax; imposes a state estate tax of up to 15 % but not less than the federal credit for state death taxes.

OREGON

State Law Description: Oregon Revised Statutes; Sections 112.015+, 115.000+, 117.000+.

Court With Probate Jurisdiction: Circuit or County Court.

Minimum Age for Disposing of Property by Will: 18 or married (any age).

Required Number of Witnesses: Two. (Three recommended.)

May Witnesses Be Beneficiaries?: Yes. (Not recommended.)

Are There Provisions for Self-Proving Wills?: Yes. (Use the Affidavit in Chapter 13.)

Are Living Wills Recognized?: Yes, under the "Oregon Patient Self Determination Act."

How Does Divorce Affect the Will?: Revokes the will as to the divorced spouse.

How Does Marriage Affect the Will?: Revokes the will if the maker of the will is survived by a spouse.

Who Must Be Mentioned in the Will?: Statute contains detailed provisions regarding this matter. Please refer directly to statute text or consult an attorney if this is a critical factor.

Spouse's Right to Property Regardless of Will: The surviving spouse is entitled to 1/4 of the deceased spouse's estate.

Laws of Intestate Distribution (Distribution If Decedent Leaves No Will):

  Spouse and Children of Spouse Surviving: 1/2 to spouse and 1/2 to children or grandchildren per stirpes.

  Spouse and Children Not of Spouse Surviving: 1/2 to spouse and 1/2 to children or grandchildren per stirpes.

  Spouse, but No Children or Parent(s) Surviving: All to spouse.

  Spouse and Parent(s), but No Children Surviving: All to spouse.

  Children, but No Spouse Surviving: All to children equally or to their children per stirpes.

  Parent(s), but No Spouse or Children Surviving: All to parents equally, or to the surviving parent.

  No Spouse, Children or Parent(s) Surviving: All to brothers and sisters equally, or their children per stirpes; or if none, to the next of kin.

Forms of Property Ownership: Common law state. Tenancy in common and tenancy by entirety recognized. Right of survivorship must be stated.

State Restrictions on Gifts to Charities?: No.

State Gift, Inheritance or Estate Taxes: No gift tax; no inheritance tax; imposes state estate tax equal to federal credit for state death taxes.

PENNSYLVANIA

State Law Description: Pennsylvania Consolidated Statutes; Title 20, Sections 101+.

Court With Probate Jurisdiction: Court of Common Pleas.

Minimum Age for Disposing of Property by Will: 18.

Required Number of Witnesses: Three.

May Witnesses Be Beneficiaries?: Yes. (Not recommended.)

Are There Provisions for Self-Proving Wills?: Yes. (Use the Affidavit in Chapter 13.)

Are Living Wills Recognized?: Yes, under "Advance Directive for Health Care Act."

How Does Divorce Affect the Will?: Revokes the will as to the divorced spouse.

How Does Marriage Affect the Will?: Revokes the will as to the spouse if she or he is not otherwise provided for. Spouse may still be entitled to her or his statutory share under the state intestate laws.

Who Must Be Mentioned in the Will?: Children, born or adopted; surviving spouse.

Spouse's Right to Property Regardless of Will: The surviving spouse is entitled to 1/3 of the deceased spouse's estate.

Laws of Intestate Distribution (Distribution If Decedent Leaves No Will):

Spouse and Children of Spouse Surviving: $30,000 and 1/2 of balance to spouse and 1/2 of balance to children or grandchildren per stirpes.

Spouse and Children Not of Spouse Surviving: 1/2 to spouse and 1/2 to children or grandchildren per stirpes.

Spouse, but No Children or Parent(s) Surviving: All to spouse.

Spouse and Parent(s), but No Children Surviving: $30,000 and 1/2 of balance to spouse and 1/2 of balance to parents or surviving parent.

Children, but No Spouse Surviving: All to children equally or to their children per stirpes.

Parent(s), but No Spouse or Children Surviving: All to parents equally, or to the surviving parent.

No Spouse, Children or Parent(s) Surviving: All to brothers and sisters equally, or their children per stirpes; or if none, 1/2 to maternal and 1/2 to paternal grandparents; or if none, all to aunts and uncles or their children per stirpes.

Forms of Property Ownership: Common law state. Tenancy in common and tenancy by entirety recognized. Joint tenancy with right of survivorship only if stated. Real estate jointly owned by spouses presumes tenancy by entirety unless stated otherwise. Tenancy by entirety in personal property recognized.

State Restrictions on Gifts to Charities?: No.

State Gift, Inheritance or Estate Taxes: No gift tax; imposes an inheritance tax of up to 15%; imposes state estate tax equal to federal credit for state death taxes less any amounts paid on state inheritance tax. Maximum total state inheritance and state estate tax is equal to the maximum allowable federal estate tax credit for state death taxes.

RHODE ISLAND
State Law Description: Rhode Island General Laws; Title 33, Chapters 33-5-1+.
Court With Probate Jurisdiction: Probate Court.
Minimum Age for Disposing of Property by Will: 18.
Required Number of Witnesses: Two. (Three recommended.)
May Witnesses Be Beneficiaries?: No.
Are There Provisions for Self-Proving Wills?: Yes. (Use the Affidavit in Chapter 13.)
Are Living Wills Recognized?: Yes, under the "Rhode Island Rights of the Terminally Ill Act."
How Does Divorce Affect the Will?: Does not revoke the will.
How Does Marriage Affect the Will?: Revokes the will completely.
Who Must Be Mentioned in the Will?: Children, born or adopted; grandchildren (if of deceased child); surviving spouse.
Spouse's Right to Property Regardless of Will: The surviving spouse is entitled to 1/3 of the deceased spouse's real estate for the rest of his or her life.
Laws of Intestate Distribution (Distribution If Decedent Leaves No Will):
　　Spouse and Children of Spouse Surviving: Real estate: life estate to spouse and balance to children equally or grandchildren per stirpes; Personal property: 1/2 to spouse and 1/2 to children or grandchildren per stirpes.
　　Spouse and Children Not of Spouse Surviving: Same as above for "Spouse and Children of Spouse Surviving."
　　Spouse, but No Children or Parent(s) Surviving: Real estate: life estate and $75,000 to spouse (if court approves), balance to brothers and sisters equally; or if none, 1/2 to maternal and 1/2 to paternal grandparents; or if none, to aunts and uncles equally or their children per stirpes; or if none, to the next of kin; or if none, to the spouse. Personal property: $50,000 and 1/2 of balance to spouse and 1/2 of balance same as for real estate.
　　Spouse and Parent(s), but No Children Surviving: Real estate: life estate and $75,000 to spouse (if court approves), balance to parents or surviving parent; personal property: $50,000 and 1/2 of balance to spouse and 1/2 of balance to parents or surviving parent.
　　Children, but No Spouse Surviving: All to children or grandchildren per stirpes.
　　Parent(s), but No Spouse or Children Surviving: All to parents equally, or to surviving parent.
　　No Spouse, Children or Parent(s) Surviving: All to brothers and sisters equally, or their children per stirpes; or if none, 1/2 to maternal and 1/2 to paternal grandparents; or if none, to the next of kin.
Forms of Property Ownership: Common law state. Tenancy in common presumed unless stated otherwise. Tenancy in common, joint tenancy and tenancy by entirety recognized.
State Restrictions on Gifts to Charities?: No.
State Gift, Inheritance or Estate Taxes: No gift tax; no inheritance tax; imposes state estate tax equal to federal credit for state death taxes.

SOUTH CAROLINA

State Law Description: Code of Laws of South Carolina Annotated; Sections 14-23-10+, 21-7-10+.
Court With Probate Jurisdiction: Probate Court.
Minimum Age for Disposing of Property by Will: 18.
Required Number of Witnesses: Three.
May Witnesses Be Beneficiaries?: Generally, yes. (Not recommended.)
Are There Provisions for Self-Proving Wills?: Yes. (Use the Affidavit in Chapter 13.)
Are Living Wills Recognized?: Yes, under the "South Carolina Death With Dignity Act."
How Does Divorce Affect the Will?: Revokes the will as to the divorced spouse.
How Does Marriage Affect the Will?: Revokes the will if spouse, children, or grandchildren survive the maker of the will.
Who Must Be Mentioned in the Will?: Children, born or adopted; surviving spouse.
Spouse's Right to Property Regardless of Will: The surviving spouse is entitled to 1/3 of the deceased spouse's real estate for the rest of his or her life.
Laws of Intestate Distribution (Distribution If Decedent Leaves No Will):
  Spouse and Children of Spouse Surviving: If only one child surviving, 1/2 to spouse and 1/2 to child or grandchildren; if more than one child surviving, 1/3 to spouse and 2/3 to children equally or their grandchildren per stirpes.
  Spouse and Children Not of Spouse Surviving: If only one child surviving, 1/2 to spouse and 1/2 to child or grandchildren; if more than one child surviving, 1/3 to spouse and 2/3 to children equally or their grandchildren per stirpes.
  Spouse, but No Children or Parent(s) Surviving: 1/2 to spouse and 1/2 to brothers and sisters per stirpes; or if none, to lineal ancestors; or if none, to spouse.
  Spouse and Parent(s), but No Children Surviving: 1/2 to spouse and 1/2 to parents, brothers, and sisters or their children per stirpes.
  Children, but No Spouse Surviving: All to children equally or to their children per stirpes.
  Parent(s), but No Spouse or Children Surviving: All to parents equally, or to the surviving parent if no brothers and sisters.
  No Spouse, Children or Parent(s) Surviving: All to brothers and sisters equally, or their children per stirpes; or if none, to lineal ancestors equally or to survivor; or if none, to aunts and uncles equally or their children per stirpes; or if none, to the next of kin.
Forms of Property Ownership: Common law state. Tenancy in common and joint tenancy recognized. Right of survivorship only if stated. No tenancy by entirety.
State Restrictions on Gifts to Charities?: No.
State Gift, Inheritance or Estate Taxes: Imposes a gift tax; no inheritance tax; imposes a state estate tax of up to 8 % but not less than the federal credit for state death taxes.

SOUTH DAKOTA

State Law Description: South Dakota Codified Laws Annotated; Title 29, Chapters 29-2-1 to 29-6-25, Title 30, Chapters 30-1-1+.
Court With Probate Jurisdiction: Circuit Court.
Minimum Age for Disposing of Property by Will: 18.
Required Number of Witnesses: Two. (Three recommended.)
May Witnesses Be Beneficiaries?: No.
Are There Provisions for Self-Proving Wills?: Yes. (Use the Affidavit in Chapter 13.)
Are Living Wills Recognized?: Yes, under the "South Dakota Living Will Act."
How Does Divorce Affect the Will?: Does not revoke the will.
How Does Marriage Affect the Will?: Revokes the will if spouse, child, or grandchildren survive the maker of the will.
Who Must Be Mentioned in the Will?: Statute contains detailed provisions regarding this matter. Please refer directly to statute or consult an attorney if this is important.
Spouse's Right to Property Regardless of Will: The surviving spouse is entitled to 1/3 of the entire "augmented" estate of the deceased spouse (essentially, all of the property of the decedent).
Laws of Intestate Distribution (Distribution If Decedent Leaves No Will):
> *Spouse and Children of Spouse Surviving:* If one child surviving, 1/2 to spouse and 1/2 to child or grandchildren; if more than one child surviving, 1/3 to spouse and 2/3 to child ren or grandchildren per stirpes.
> *Spouse and Children Not of Spouse Surviving:* Same as above for "Spouse and Children of Spouse Surviving."
> *Spouse, but No Children or Parent(s) Surviving:* $100,000 and 1/2 of balance to spouse, 1/2 of balance to brothers and sisters equally or their children per stirpes; or if none, to the spouse.
> *Spouse and Parent(s), but No Children Surviving:* $100,000 and 1/2 of balance to spouse, 1/2 of balance to parents or the surviving parent.
> *Children, but No Spouse Surviving:* All to children or to their children per stirpes.
> *Parent(s), but No Spouse or Children Surviving:* All to parents equally, or to the surviving parent.
> *No Spouse, Children or Parent(s) Surviving:* All to brothers and sisters equally, or their children per stirpes; or if none, to the next of kin.
Forms of Property Ownership: Common law state. Tenancy in common and joint tenancy recognized. No tenancy by entirety. Creditors' rights preserved against surviving joint owner(s).
State Restrictions on Gifts to Charities?: No.
State Gift, Inheritance or Estate Taxes: No gift tax; imposes an inheritance tax of up to 30%; imposes state estate tax equal to federal credit for state death taxes less any amounts paid on state inheritance tax. Maximum total state inheritance and state estate tax is equal to the maximum allowable federal estate tax credit for state death taxes.

TENNESSEE

State Law Description: Tennessee Code Annotated; Title 30, Sections 30-1-101+; Title 32, Sections 32-1-101+.
Court With Probate Jurisdiction: Chancery Court. (Probate Court in Davidson and Shelby Counties.)
Minimum Age for Disposing of Property by Will: 18.
Required Number of Witnesses: Two. (Three recommended.)
May Witnesses Be Beneficiaries?: No.
Are There Provisions for Self-Proving Wills?: Yes. (Use the Affidavit in Chapter 13.)
Are Living Wills Recognized?: Yes, under the "Tennessee Right to Natural Death Act."
How Does Divorce Affect the Will?: Revokes the will as to the divorced spouse.
How Does Marriage Affect the Will?: Revokes the will if a child is later born to the marriage.
Who Must Be Mentioned in the Will?: Children, born or adopted; surviving spouse.
Spouse's Right to Property Regardless of Will: The surviving spouse is entitled to 1/3 of the deceased spouse's estate.
Laws of Intestate Distribution (Distribution If Decedent Leaves No Will):
  Spouse and Children of Spouse Surviving: Family homestead and one year's support allowance and one child's share of estate (at least 1/3) to spouse, balance to children equally or grandchildren per stirpes.
  Spouse and Children Not of Spouse Surviving: Family homestead and one year's support allowance and one child's share of estate (at least 1/3) to spouse, balance to children equally or grandchildren per stirpes.
  Spouse, but No Children or Parent(s) Surviving: All to spouse.
  Spouse and Parent(s), but No Children Surviving: All to spouse.
  Children, but No Spouse Surviving: All to children equally or to their children per stirpes.
  Parent(s), but No Spouse or Children Surviving: All to parents equally, or to the surviving parent.
  No Spouse, Children or Parent(s) Surviving: All to brothers and sisters equally, or their children per stirpes; or if none, 1/2 to maternal and 1/2 to paternal grandparents or surviving grandparent; or if none, to the children of grandparents per stirpes.
Forms of Property Ownership: Common law state. Tenancy in common and tenancy by entirety recognized.
State Restrictions on Gifts to Charities?: No.
State Gift, Inheritance or Estate Taxes: Imposes a gift tax; imposes an inheritance tax of up to 16%; imposes state estate tax equal to federal credit for state death taxes less any amounts paid on state inheritance tax. Maximum total state inheritance and state estate tax is equal to the maximum allowable federal estate tax credit for state death taxes.

TEXAS

State Law Description: Texas Statutes and Code Annotated; Probate Title, Chapters 1+.

Court With Probate Jurisdiction: County or Probate Court.

Minimum Age for Disposing of Property by Will: 18, or married (any age), or member of Armed Forces (any age).

Required Number of Witnesses: Two. (Three recommended.)

May Witnesses Be Beneficiaries?: Generally, yes. (Not recommended.)

Are There Provisions for Self-Proving Wills?: Yes. (A locally drafted self-proving affidavit is advised.)

Are Living Wills Recognized?: Yes, under the "Texas Natural Death Act."

How Does Divorce Affect the Will?: Revokes the will as to the divorced spouse.

How Does Marriage Affect the Will?: Does not revoke the will.

Who Must Be Mentioned in the Will?: Children, born or adopted.

Spouse's Right to Property Regardless of Will: Community property right to 1/2 of the deceased spouse's "community" property.

Laws of Intestate Distribution (Distribution If Decedent Leaves No Will):

> **Spouse and Children of Spouse Surviving:** 1/2 of community property, 1/3 life estate in separate real property, and 1/3 separate personal property to spouse; balance to children or grandchildren per stirpes.

> **Spouse and Children Not of Spouse Surviving:** Same as above for "Spouse and Children of Spouse Surviving."

> **Spouse, but No Children or Parent(s) Surviving:** All community property, all separate personal property and 1/2 separate real property to spouse; balance to brothers and sisters equally or their children per stirpes; or if none, to grandparents or their descendants; or if none, to spouse.

> **Spouse and Parent(s), but No Children Surviving:** All community property, all separate personal property and 1/2 separate real property to spouse; balance to parents (if both surviving); if only one surviving, 1/4 balance to parent and 1/4 to brothers and sisters equally or their children per stirpes; or if none, entire 1/2 to parent.

> **Children, but No Spouse Surviving:** All to children or to their children per stirpes.

> **Parent(s), but No Spouse or Children Surviving:** If both parents are surviving, all to parents equally; if only one surviving, 1/2 to parent and 1/2 to brothers and sisters equally or their children per stirpes; or if none, all to parent.

> **No Spouse, Children or Parent(s) Surviving:** All to brothers and sisters equally, or their children per stirpes; or if none, 1/2 to maternal and 1/2 to paternal grandparents or their children per stirpes.

Forms of Property Ownership: Community property state. All property acquired by either spouse during marriage is community property. Tenancy in common recognized. No tenancy by entirety.

State Restrictions on Gifts to Charities?: No.

State Gift, Inheritance or Estate Taxes: No gift tax; no inheritance tax; imposes state estate tax equal to federal credit for state death taxes.

UTAH

State Law Description: Utah Code Annotated; Sections 75-2-101+.

Court With Probate Jurisdiction: District Court.

Minimum Age for Disposing of Property by Will: 18.

Required Number of Witnesses: Two. (Three recommended.)

May Witnesses Be Beneficiaries?: Yes. (Not recommended.)

Are There Provisions for Self-Proving Wills?: Yes. (Use the Affidavit in Chapter 13.)

Are Living Wills Recognized?: Yes, under the "Utah Personal Choice and Living Will Act."

How Does Divorce Affect the Will?: Revokes the will as to the divorced spouse.

How Does Marriage Affect the Will?: Revokes the will as to the spouse if she or he is not otherwise provided for. Spouse may still be entitled to her or his statutory share under the state intestate laws.

Who Must Be Mentioned in the Will?: Children, born or adopted; grandchildren (if of deceased child); surviving spouse.

Spouse's Right to Property Regardless of Will: The surviving spouse is entitled to 1/3 of the deceased spouse's estate.

Laws of Intestate Distribution (Distribution If Decedent Leaves No Will):

   Spouse and Children of Spouse Surviving: $50,000 and 1/2 of balance to spouse and 1/2 of balance to children or grandchildren per stirpes.

   Spouse and Children Not of Spouse Surviving: 1/2 to spouse and 1/2 to children or grandchildren per stirpes.

   Spouse, but No Children or Parent(s) Surviving: All to spouse.

   Spouse and Parent(s), but No Children Surviving: $100,000 and 1/2 of balance to spouse and 1/2 to parents or surviving parent.

   Children, but No Spouse Surviving: All to children equally or to their children per stirpes.

   Parent(s), but No Spouse or Children Surviving: All to parents equally, or to the surviving parent.

   No Spouse, Children or Parent(s) Surviving: All to brothers and sisters equally, or their children per stirpes; 1/2 to maternal and 1/2 to paternal grandparents or their descendants per stirpes; or if none, to the next of kin.

Forms of Property Ownership: Common law state. Tenancy in common, joint tenancy and tenancy by entirety recognized. Real estate presumed to be in tenancy in common. Joint tenancy only if stated.

State Restrictions on Gifts to Charities?: No.

State Gift, Inheritance or Estate Taxes: No gift tax; no inheritance tax; imposes state estate tax equal to federal credit for state death taxes.

VERMONT

State Law Description: Vermont Statutes Annotated; Sections Title 14, Sections 1+.

Court With Probate Jurisdiction: Probate Court.

Minimum Age for Disposing of Property by Will: 18.

Required Number of Witnesses: Three.

May Witnesses Be Beneficiaries?: No.

Are There Provisions for Self-Proving Wills?: Not in statutes. However self-proving affidavits have been accepted in the courts. (Use the Affidavit in Chapter 13.)

Are Living Wills Recognized?: Yes, under the "Vermont Terminal Care Document Act."

How Does Divorce Affect the Will?: Does not revoke the will.

How Does Marriage Affect the Will?: Does not revoke the will.

Who Must Be Mentioned in the Will?: Children, born or adopted; grandchildren (if of deceased child); surviving spouse.

Spouse's Right to Property Regardless of Will: The surviving spouse is entitled to 1/3 of the deceased spouse's real estate for the rest of his or her life.

Laws of Intestate Distribution (Distribution If Decedent Leaves No Will):

    Spouse and Children of Spouse Surviving: If one child surviving: 1/2 of real estate and 1/3 of personal property to spouse; balance to child or grandchildren per stirpes. If more than one child surviving: 1/3 to spouse and 2/3 to children or grandchildren per stirpes.

    Spouse and Children Not of Spouse Surviving: If one child surviving: 1/2 of real estate and 1/3 of personal property to spouse; balance to child or grandchildren per stirpes. If more than one child surviving: 1/3 to spouse and 2/3 to children or grandchildren per stirpes.

    Spouse, but No Children or Parent(s) Surviving: $25,000 and 1/2 of balance to spouse and 1/2 of balance to brothers and sisters equally or their children per stirpes; or if none, to the next of kin; or if none, to the spouse.

    Spouse and Parent(s), but No Children Surviving: $25,000 and 1/2 of balance to spouse and 1/2 of balance to parents or surviving parent.

    Children, but No Spouse Surviving: All to children equally or to their children per stirpes.

    Parent(s), but No Spouse or Children Surviving: All to parents equally, or to the surviving parent.

    No Spouse, Children or Parent(s) Surviving: All to brothers and sisters equally, or their children per stirpes; or if none, to the next of kin.

Forms of Property Ownership: Common law state. Tenancy in common, tenancy by entirety and joint tenancy recognized. The presumption is real estate is held by tenancy in common rather than joint tenancy unless otherwise stated.

State Restrictions on Gifts to Charities?: No.

State Gift, Inheritance or Estate Taxes: No gift tax; no inheritance tax; imposes state estate tax equal to federal credit for state death taxes.

VIRGINIA

State Law Description: Virginia Code Annotated; Title 64, Sections 64.1-1 to 64.1-180.
Court With Probate Jurisdiction: Circuit Court.
Minimum Age for Disposing of Property by Will: 18.
Required Number of Witnesses: Two. (Three recommended.)
May Witnesses Be Beneficiaries?: No.
Are There Provisions for Self-Proving Wills?: Yes. (Use the Affidavit in Chapter 13.)
Are Living Wills Recognized?: Yes, under the "Virginia Natural Death Act."
How Does Divorce Affect the Will?: Revokes the will as to the divorced spouse.
How Does Marriage Affect the Will?: Does not revoke the will.
Who Must Be Mentioned in the Will?: Children, born or adopted; grandchildren (if of deceased child); surviving spouse.
Spouse's Right to Property Regardless of Will: The surviving spouse is entitled to 1/3 of the deceased spouse's real estate for the rest of his or her life.
Laws of Intestate Distribution (Distribution If Decedent Leaves No Will):
　Spouse and Children of Spouse Surviving: All to spouse.
　Spouse and Children Not of Spouse Surviving: 1/3 to spouse and 2/3 to children or grandchildren per stirpes.
　Spouse, but No Children or Parent(s) Surviving: All to spouse.
　Spouse and Parent(s), but No Children Surviving: All to spouse.
　Children, but No Spouse Surviving: All to children equally or to their children per stirpes.
　Parent(s), but No Spouse or Children Surviving: All to parents equally, or to the surviving parent.
　No Spouse, Children or Parent(s) Surviving: All to brothers and sisters equally, or their children per stirpes; or if none, 1/2 to maternal grandparents or maternal next of kin (or if none, to paternal side) and 1/2 to paternal grandparents, or their children, or paternal next of kin (or if none to maternal side).
Forms of Property Ownership: Common law state. Joint tenancy only where right of survivorship is stated. Tenancy in common and tenancy by entirety recognized.
State Restrictions on Gifts to Charities?: No.
State Gift, Inheritance or Estate Taxes: No gift tax; no inheritance tax; imposes state estate tax equal to federal credit for state death taxes.

WASHINGTON

State Law Description: Washington Revised Code Annotated; Title 11, Chapters 11.02.001+, 11.12.010+ .

Court With Probate Jurisdiction: Superior Court.

Minimum Age for Disposing of Property by Will: 18.

Required Number of Witnesses: Two. (Three recommended.)

May Witnesses Be Beneficiaries?: No.

Are There Provisions for Self-Proving Wills?: Yes. (Use the Affidavit in Chapter 13.)

Are Living Wills Recognized?: Yes, under the "Washington Natural Death Act."

How Does Divorce Affect the Will?: Revokes the will as to the divorced spouse.

How Does Marriage Affect the Will?: Revokes the will as to the surviving spouse.

Who Must Be Mentioned in the Will?: Statute contains detailed provisions regarding this matter. Please refer directly to statute text or consult an attorney if this is a critical factor.

Spouse's Right to Property Regardless of Will: Community property right to 1/2 of the deceased spouse's "community" property.

Laws of Intestate Distribution (Distribution If Decedent Leaves No Will):

    Spouse and Children of Spouse Surviving: All of decedent's community property and 1/2 of decedent's separate property to spouse; 1/2 of decedent's separate property to children or grandchildren per stirpes.

    Spouse and Children Not of Spouse Surviving: All of decedent's community property and 1/2 of decedent's separate property to spouse; 1/2 of decedent's separate property to children or grandchildren per stirpes.

    Spouse, but No Children or Parent(s) Surviving: All to spouse.

    Spouse and Parent(s), but No Children Surviving: All decedent's community property and 3/4 decedent's separate property to spouse; 1/4 decedent's separate property to parents or surviving parent or their children.

    Children, but No Spouse Surviving: All to children equally or to their children per stirpes.

    Parent(s), but No Spouse or Children Surviving: All to parents equally, or to the surviving parent.

    No Spouse, Children or Parent(s) Surviving: All to brothers and sisters equally, or their children per stirpes; or if none, to grandparents or their children.

Forms of Property Ownership: Common law state. Joint tenancy only where right of survivorship is stated. Tenancy in common and tenancy by entirety recognized.

State Restrictions on Gifts to Charities?: No.

State Gift, Inheritance or Estate Taxes: No gift tax; no inheritance tax; imposes state estate tax equal to federal credit for state death taxes.

WEST VIRGINIA

State Law Description: West Virginia Code Annotated; Sections 41, 42, 44-1-1.

Court With Probate Jurisdiction: County Commissioner.

Minimum Age for Disposing of Property by Will: 18.

Required Number of Witnesses: Two. (Three recommended.)

May Witnesses Be Beneficiaries?: No.

Are There Provisions for Self-Proving Wills?: Yes. (Use the Affidavit in Chapter 13.)

Are Living Wills Recognized?: Yes, under the "West Virginia Natural Death Act."

How Does Divorce Affect the Will?: Revokes the will completely.

How Does Marriage Affect the Will?: Revokes the will completely.

Who Must Be Mentioned in the Will?: Children, born or adopted; grandchildren; surviving spouse.

Spouse's Right to Property Regardless of Will: The surviving spouse is entitled to 1/3 of the deceased spouse's real estate for the rest of his or her life.

Laws of Intestate Distribution (Distribution If Decedent Leaves No Will):

Spouse and Children of Spouse Surviving: 3/5 to spouse; balance to children or grandchildren by representation.

Spouse and Children Not of Spouse Surviving: 1/2 to spouse; balance to children or grandchildren by representation.

Spouse, but No Children or Parent(s) Surviving: All to spouse.

Spouse and Parent(s), but No Children Surviving: 3/4 to spouse.

Children, but No Spouse Surviving: All to children equally or to their children by representation.

Parent(s), but No Spouse or Children Surviving: All to parents equally, or to the surviving parent.

No Spouse, Children or Parent(s) Surviving: All to parent's descendants by representation; or if none, 1/2 to maternal grandparents or their descendants by representation.

Forms of Property Ownership: Common law state. Joint tenancy only where right of survivorship is stated. Tenancy in common and tenancy by entirety recognized.

State Restrictions on Gifts to Charities?: No.

State Gift, Inheritance or Estate Taxes: No gift tax; no inheritance tax; imposes state estate tax equal to federal credit for state death taxes.

WISCONSIN

State Law Description: Wisconsin Statutes Annotated; Sections 851.001+, 853.01+

Court With Probate Jurisdiction: Circuit Court.

Minimum Age for Disposing of Property by Will: 18.

Required Number of Witnesses: Two. (Three recommended.)

May Witnesses Be Beneficiaries?: No.

Are There Provisions for Self-Proving Wills?: Not in statutes. However self-proving affidavits have been accepted in the courts. (Use the Affidavit in Chapter 13.)

Are Living Wills Recognized?: Yes, under the "Wisconsin Natural Death Act."

How Does Divorce Affect the Will?: Revokes the will as to the divorced spouse.

How Does Marriage Affect the Will?: Revokes the will as to the spouse if she or he is not otherwise provided for. Spouse may still be entitled to her or his statutory share under the state intestate laws.

Who Must Be Mentioned in the Will?: Children, born or adopted; grandchildren (if of deceased child); surviving spouse.

Spouse's Right to Property Regardless of Will: Modified community property right to 1/2 of the deceased spouse's "community" property.

Laws of Intestate Distribution (Distribution If Decedent Leaves No Will):

   Spouse and Children of Spouse Surviving: All to spouse.

   Spouse and Children Not of Spouse Surviving: 1/2 to spouse and 1/2 to children or grandchildren per stirpes.

   Spouse, but No Children or Parent(s) Surviving: All to spouse.

   Spouse and Parent(s), but No Children Surviving: All to spouse.

   Children, but No Spouse Surviving: All to children or to their children per stirpes.

   Parent(s), but No Spouse or Children Surviving: All to parents equally, or to the surviving parent.

   No Spouse, Children or Parent(s) Surviving: All to brothers and sisters equally, or their children per stirpes; or if none, to grandparents or surviving grandparent; or if none, to the next of kin.

Forms of Property Ownership: Community property state. Tenancy in common and joint tenancy recognized. Ownership by spouses presumes joint tenancy unless document states otherwise. No tenancy by entirety.

State Restrictions on Gifts to Charities?: No.

State Gift, Inheritance or Estate Taxes: Imposes a gift tax; imposes an inheritance tax of up to 20%; imposes state estate tax equal to federal credit for state death taxes less any amounts paid on state inheritance tax. Maximum total state inheritance and state estate tax is equal to the maximum allowable federal estate tax credit for state death taxes.

Note: Fill-in-the-blank statutory will forms available from probate court and legal stationery stores.

WYOMING

State Law Description: Wyoming Statutes; Title 2, Chapters 2-1-101+.
Court With Probate Jurisdiction: District Court.
Minimum Age for Disposing of Property by Will: 18.
Required Number of Witnesses: Two. (Three recommended.)
May Witnesses Be Beneficiaries?: No.
Are There Provisions for Self-Proving Wills?: Yes. (Use the Affidavit in Chapter 13.)
Are Living Wills Recognized?: Yes, under the "Wyoming Living Will Act."
How Does Divorce Affect the Will?: Revokes the will as to the divorced spouse.
How Does Marriage Affect the Will?: Does not revoke the will.
Who Must Be Mentioned in the Will?: Statute contains detailed provisions regarding this matter. Please refer directly to statute text or consult an attorney if this is a critical factor.
Spouse's Right to Property Regardless of Will: Generally, the surviving spouse is entitled to 1/2 of the deceased spouse's estate if there are no children, and only 1/3 if there are children. However, please refer directly to the statute as the provisions are detailed.
Laws of Intestate Distribution (Distribution If Decedent Leaves No Will):
  Spouse and Children of Spouse Surviving: 1/2 to spouse and 1/2 to children or grandchildren per stirpes.
  Spouse and Children Not of Spouse Surviving: 1/2 to spouse and 1/2 to children or grandchildren per stirpes.
  Spouse, but No Children or Parent(s) Surviving: All to spouse.
  Spouse and Parent(s), but No Children Surviving: All to spouse.
  Children, but No Spouse Surviving: All to children equally or to their children per stirpes.
  Parent(s), but No Spouse or Children Surviving: All to parents, brothers, and sisters equally, or to children of brothers and sisters per stirpes.
  No Spouse, Children or Parent(s) Surviving: All to brothers and sisters equally, or their children per stirpes; or if none, to grandparents, uncles, or aunts or their children per stirpes.
Forms of Property Ownership: Common law state. Tenancy in common, joint tenancy and tenancy by entirety recognized. Right of survivorship created if stated.
State Restrictions on Gifts to Charities?: No.
State Gift, Inheritance or Estate Taxes: No gift tax; no inheritance tax; imposes state estate tax equal to federal credit for state death taxes.

UNIFIED FEDERAL ESTATE & GIFT TAX RATES

The following chart gives the unified federal estate and gift tax rates for estates of people who have died after 1987. As discussed in Chapter 9, these taxes don't kick in unless your taxable estate is worth $600,000 or more. In order to calculate the tax owed, first you must determine your taxable estate – your net worth minus liabilities and exempt amounts (funeral expenses, charitable gifts, any amount left to a surviving spouse). Then, check on the chart below for the tax owed on the taxable estate. Finally, subtract the tax credit for the amount that would be owed on the first $600,000 (about $192,000). Remember, this credit may be lower if you have given gifts of more than $10,000 per year per person during your life.

1	2	3	4
If taxable estate is more than	But not more than	Tax owed on amounts in 1	Rate of tax on excess over amounts in 1
$ 0	$ 10,000	$ 0	18%
10,000	20,000	1,800	20
20,000	40,000	3,800	22
40,000	60,000	8,200	24
60,000	80,000	13,000	26
80,000	100,000	18,200	28
100,000	150,000	23,800	30
150,000	250,000	38,800	32
250,000	500,000	70,800	34
500,000	750,000	155,800	37
750,000	1,000,000	248,300	39
1,000,000	1,250,000	345,800	41
1,250,000	1,500,000	448,300	43
1,500,000	2,000,000	555,800	45
2,000,000	2,500,000	780,800	49
2,500,000	–	1,025,800	50

Appendix III:

PROPERTY INVENTORY

Date of Preparation
_____

I. FAMILY INFORMATION

You   Spouse

Name
_____ | _____

Address
_____ | _____

Phone Number
_____ | _____

Birth Date
_____ | _____

Social Security Number
_____ | _____

Employer
_____ | _____

Address/Phone Number
_____ | _____

Child(ren) (include address)

	Birth Date	Social Security Number
1.		
2.		
3.		
4.		

Grandchild(ren)/Other Dependents (include address)

	Birth Date	Social Security Number
1.		
2.		
3.		
4.		

Your Parents	Your Spouse's Parents
Name	
Address	
Phone Number	

II. IMPORTANT FAMILY CONTACTS (include name, address and phone number)

Lawyer _____

Accountant _____

Bank Officer _____

Clergy _____

Doctor _____

Insurance Agent _____

Stock Broker _____

Closest Relative _____

Neighbor _____

Funeral Director _____

III. FINANCIAL INFORMATION

A. YOUR ASSETS

Real Estate (land, home, business property, condos, co-ops, etc.)

Description or Address	Type of Ownership (sole, joint, etc.)	Market Value/Equity

Cash or Equivalent Funds (checking, savings, money market, certificates of deposit, etc.)

Type	Bank	Account Number	Type of Ownership

Investments (stocks, bonds, mutual funds, other securities, etc.)

Type	Company	Number of Shares	Market Value

Personal Possessions (list most valuable items, such as cars, jewelry, furniture, heirlooms, etc.)

Description, Location and Value

Retirement Plans (IRAs, pension plans, Keoghs, etc.)

Type	Name of Plan	Beneficiary	Current Value

Life Insurance (also note the policy number and type of insurance coverage, such as whole or term)

Insured	Company	Beneficiary	Death Benefit

Debts Owed You (include name, address and phone number)

Who Owes	Amount Owed

B. *YOUR LIABILITIES*

Type	Company/Person Owed	Amount Owed	When Due	Secured By
Mortgages				
Installment loans				
Education loans				
Personal loans				
Other debts				

C. FIGURING OUT YOUR NET WORTH

Amounts

	You	Spouse	Joint
ASSETS			
Real estate			
Cash or Equivalent Funds			
Investments			
Personal Possessions			
Retirement Plans			
Life Insurance			
Debts Owed You			
Total Assets			
LIABILITIES			
Mortgages			
Installment Loans			
Education Loans			
Personal Loans			
Other Debts			
Total Liabilities			
NET ESTATE (assets minus liabilities)			

IV. WILL DECISIONS (fill in names, addresses and telephone numbers for each)

Executor _____

Alternate Executor _____

Child(ren)'s Guardian _____

Alternate Child(ren)'s Guardian _____

Child(ren)'s Trustee _____

Alternate Child(ren)'s Trustee _____

V. PROPERTY DISTRIBUTION

Gifts of Personal Property to:

Name _____

Address _____

Telephone _____

Specific Property Given _____

Alternate Beneficiary _____

Alt. Benef. Address _____

Name _____

Address _____

Telephone _____

Specific Property Given _____

Alternate Beneficiary _____

Alt. Benef. Address _____

Name _____

Address _____

Telephone _____

Specific Property Given _____

Alternate Beneficiary _____

Alt. Benef. Address _____

Name _____

Address _____

Telephone _____

Specific Property Given _____

Alternate Beneficiary _____

Alt. Benef. Address _____

Gifts of Real Property to:

Name _____

Address _____

Telephone _____

Specific Property Given _____

Alternate Beneficiary _____

Alt. Benef. Address _____

Name _____

Address _____

Telephone _____

Specific Property Given _____

Alternate Beneficiary _____

Alt. Benef. Address _____

Name _____

Address _____

Telephone _____

Specific Property Given _____

Alternate Beneficiary _____

Alt. Benef. Address _____

Name _____

Address _____

Telephone _____

Specific Property Given _____

Alternate Beneficiary _____

Alt. Benef. Address _____

General Gifts of Money to:

Name _____

Address _____

Telephone _____

Specific Amount Given _____

Alternate Beneficiary _____

Alt. Benef. Address _____

Name _____

Address _____

Telephone _____

Specific Amount Given _____

Alternate Beneficiary _____

Alt. Benef. Address _____

Name _____

Address _____

Telephone _____

Specific Amount Given _____

Alternate Beneficiary _____

Alt. Benef. Address _____

Name _____

Address _____

Telephone _____

Specific Amount Given _____

Alternate Beneficiary _____

Alt. Benef. Address _____

Residuary Estate to (if naming one beneficiary):

Name _____

Address _____

Telephone _____

Percentage of Estate Given _____

Alternate Beneficiary(s) _____

Alt. Benef. Address(es) _____

Percentage of Estate Given _____

Residuary Estate to (more than one beneficiary):

Names _____

Addresses _____

Telephone Numbers _____

Percentage of Estate Given _____

Alternate Beneficiary(s) _____

Alt. Benef. Address(es) _____

Percentage of Estate Given _____

SAMPLE WILLS

This appendix includes three sample wills: one for an individual without children, one for an individual with children, and one for transferring leftover property (i.e., the residuary estate) to an existing revocable living trust.

Simple Will for An Individual Without Children

In this will, Mary, a single woman without children, makes three specific gifts of personal property and one specific gift of real property; she leaves her residuary estate in equal shares to all of her siblings. If none of them are able to inherit, her estate goes to her first cousin Deidre. She appoints her sister and one of her brothers to act as co-executors of her estate.

Last Will and Testament of
Mary Frances Young

I, Mary Frances Young, a resident of New Castle County in Kenton, Delaware, being of sound mind and memory and not acting under any duress, fraud or undue influence, declare this to be my Last Will and Testament.

1. I revoke all previous wills and codicils made by me.

2. I am single and do not have any children.

3. I was formerly married to Joseph Jones. Our marriage ended on February 1, 1977, by death.

4. No beneficiary in my will shall be deemed to have survived me unless living on the 30th day after my death.

Continued on Following Page

5. I make the following specific gifts of personal property:

I give all my china, crystal, and silverware to my sister Agnes if she survives me, or if not, I direct that my china, crystal, and silverware become a part of my residuary estate and be distributed accordingly.

I give my diamond earrings to my sister-in-law Julie if she survives me, or if not, to my girlfriend, Collette Farragher. If my alternate beneficiary does not survive me, I direct that my diamond earrings become a part of my residuary estate and be distributed accordingly.

I give the car I own at death to my brother Noel if he survives me, or if not, I direct that my car become a part of my residuary estate and be distributed accordingly.

6. I make the following specific gifts of real property:

I give my two bedroom condominium located at 45 Elm Street, #233, Kenton, Delaware, to my brother Liam if he survives me, or if not, I direct that my condominium become a part of my residuary estate and be distributed accordingly.

If the property identified above is subject to a mortgage, deed of trust, lien or other encumbrance at the time of my death, such encumbrances shall pass intact to the beneficiary receiving that property.

7. I give the residue of my estate in equal shares, whether real or personal and wherever situated, to my sister and brothers, Agnes, Noel and Liam if they survive me. If any of my named beneficiaries do not survive me, than his or her share shall go to my surviving beneficiaries in equal parts. If all of my beneficiaries fail to survive me, than I give the residue of my estate to my first cousin Deidre Noonan.

8. I direct my executor to find a caring home for Sly and Shy, my pet cats. Any reasonable expense associated with finding a new home for my pets are to be paid out of my residuary estate.

9. I nominate Agnes and Liam to serve as co-executors of my estate with Agnes having the right to make final decisions if disagreements arise. If one of the named executors cannot or does not serve for any reason, the remaining executor can serve alone. If both executors are unable to serve, I nominate Noel for the position. Any appointed executor shall not be required to post a bond.

Continued on Following Page

10. My executor shall have the authority to perform any act he or she thinks necessary and in the best interest of my estate and descendants, with no limitations, and consistent with the laws of Delaware. In addition, my executor is authorized to:

a. retain, until distribution and without liability for loss or depreciation resulting from such retention, any of my assets which shall come into his or her possession as a result of administering my estate.

b. mortgage, lease, pledge, exchange, partition, or sell any of my assets without prior court order, whether real or personal, at public or private sale and to invest or reinvest the proceeds from any sale in the best interest of my estate.

c. pass any real or personal property which is encumbered by a mortgage, deed of trust, lease or any other loan obligation that requires the payment of money, to the recipient of that particular property.

d. exercise or sell any or all conversion, subscription, option, voting and other rights of whatsoever nature pertaining to any such property, and in their discretion to vote, in person or by proxy, with respect to any matters regarding stocks, securities or other assets constituting part of my estate.

e. retain and continue to operate any business, incorporated or otherwise, which is a part of my estate, including the right to effectuate any plan of corporate or business reorganization, consolidation, merger or similar plan.

f. prosecute, compromise, settle or submit to arbitration any claim in favor or against my estate.

g. appoint and pay a reasonable compensation to any agent, representative or attorney hired to handle any matter concerning my estate.

h. settle my estate without intervention of any court, except to the extent required by law.

11. I direct that my executor pay all estate, inheritance and other taxes assessed against my estate, including assets passing under or outside of my will, out of my residuary estate.

Continued on Following Page

IN WITNESS WHEREOF I have signed this Will on this 3rd day of December, 1991 in Kenton, Delaware.

Mary Frances Young
(Mary Frances Young)

The forgoing instrument, consisting of four pages, including this witness page, was declared, signed and published by Mary Frances Young as her Last Will and Testament in the presence of us, who were all present at the same time, and who, in her presence and at her request, have signed our names as witnesses. We declare that to the best of our knowledge, Mary Frances Young appeared to be of legal age, of sound mind and memory and under no constraint or undue influence at the time she executed the foregoing instrument. We declare this to be true under penalty of perjury.

Alan Spencer, 151 Main Street, Hartly, DE

Matthew Garrison, 10 Pinebridge Road, Cheswood, DE

Ina Jackson, 1 Robin Lane, Blackbird, DE

Simple Will With Children's Trust

In this will, Cassandra, names her husband as guardian of their two young children. If she and her husband die before either of them reach the age of 21, her will creates a trust for each child and appoints their aunt, Anna, to act as trustee. Cassandra's residuary estate and her solely owned business go to her husband if he survives her. If not, it passes in equal share either directly to her children or to her children's trusts.

Last Will and Testament of
Cassandra Margarita Rodriguez

I, Cassandra Margarita Rodriguez, a resident of Bernalillo County in Albuquerque, New Mexico, being of sound mind and memory and not acting under any duress, fraud or undue influence, declare this to be my Last Will and Testament.

1. I revoke all previous wills and codicils made by me.

2. I am married to Carlos Rodriguez, herein referred to as my husband and together we have two children; Manuel Rodriguez born, May 7, 1977, and Pedro Rodriguez born January 20, 1982. It is my intention that my will include the above named children and any other children born to or adopted by me after the date of this will.

3. No beneficiary in my will shall be deemed to have survived me unless living on the 30th day after my death.

4. If any of my children are still minors at the time of my death, I appoint my husband to serve as guardian over their person and property. If he does not or cannot serve for any reason, I nominate my sister, Anna Rodgers for the position. No guardian shall be required to furnish bond.

Continued on Following Page

5. If any of my children are twenty-one (21) years or younger at the time of my death and my husband has predeceased me, I direct that a trust be created to hold the property given them under this will. A separate trust shall be created for each child twenty-one (21) years or younger at the time of my death. Each trust shall end when the beneficiary of that trust turns twenty-five (25) years old.

I appoint my sister Anna Rodgers to serve as trustee. If she does not or cannot serve for any reason, I nominate my brother Fernando Sanchez for the position. No trustee shall be required to give any bond or obtain the order or approval of any court in carrying out any powers or discretion granted in this trust.

The trustee and alternate trustee shall have the full power and authority allowed by the state of New Mexico to manage and distribute based on his or her sole discretion the trust's income and principal on behalf of the beneficiary, including the right to use income and/or principal for the beneficiary's education, health, including medical expenses, support and maintenance.

The trust shall terminate when: the beneficiary turns twenty-five (25) years old; the beneficiary dies; or the trust funds are exhausted through distributions allowed under the provisions of this trust, whichever happens first. Any trust funds remaining at the termination of the trust shall pass to the beneficiary, or if no longer living, to the beneficiary's heirs.

6. I make the following specific gifts of real property:

I give my business, Cassandra's Gift and Flower Shop, located at 777 Fifteenth Street, Albuquerque, New Mexico, including all its real and personal property to my husband if he survives me, or if not, I direct that my business become a part of my residuary estate and be distributed accordingly.

If the property identified above is subject to a mortgage, deed of trust, lien or other encumbrance at the time of my death, such encumbrances shall pass intact to the beneficiary receiving that property.

Continued on Following Page

7. I make the following general gifts of money:

I give the sum of $5,000 to St. Jude's Hospital of Albuquerque, New Mexico.

I give the sum of $3,000 to The University of New Mexico's Alumni Association.

8. I give the residue of my estate, whether real or personal and wherever situated, to my husband if he survives me. If my husband does not survive me, than I give the residue in equal shares; one to each of my children if they survive me. If any of my children should not survive me, I give their share to their children or issue, if they have any, per stirpes.

Notwithstanding the foregoing, if my husband predeceases me and any child of mine has not reached the age of twenty-one (21) at the time of my death, all such property to be distributed to such child shall be distributed to the trustee named herein, to be held, administered and distributed as instructed under the terms of the children's trust provision.

9. If any of my beneficiaries chooses to contest or attack my will, or any of its provisions, his or her share under this will shall be deemed revoked and distributed as if the contesting beneficiary had predeceased me without any children.

10. I nominate my husband to serve as the executor of my estate. If he does not or cannot serve for any reason, I nominate my sister Anna for the position. Any appointed executor shall not be required to post a bond.

11. My executor shall have the authority to perform any act he or she thinks necessary and in the best interest of my estate and descendants, with no limitations, and consistent with the laws of New Mexico. In addition, my executor is authorized to:

a. retain, until distribution and without liability for loss or depreciation resulting from such retention, any of my assets which shall come into his or her possession as a result of administering my estate.

b. mortgage, lease, pledge, exchange, partition, or sell any of my assets without prior court order, whether real or personal, at public or private sale and to invest or reinvest the proceeds from any sale in the best interest of my estate.

Continued on Following Page

c. pass any real or personal property which is encumbered by a mortgage, deed of trust, lease or any other loan obligation that requires the payment of money, to the recipient of that particular property.

d. exercise or sell any or all conversion, subscription, option, voting and other rights of whatsoever nature pertaining to any such property, and in their discretion to vote, in person or by proxy, with respect to any matters regarding stocks, securities or other assets constituting part of my estate.

e. retain and continue to operate any business, incorporated or otherwise, which is a part of my estate, including the right to effectuate any plan of corporate or business reorganization, consolidation, merger or similar plan.

f. prosecute, compromise, settle or submit to arbitration any claim in favor or against my estate.

g. appoint and pay a reasonable compensation to any agent, representative or attorney hired to handle any matter concerning my estate.

h. settle my estate without intervention of any court, except to the extent required by law.

12. I direct that my executor pay all estate, inheritance and other taxes assessed against my estate, including assets passing under or outside of my will, out of my residuary estate.

Continued on Following Page

IN WITNESS WHEREOF I have signed this Will on this 12th day of April, 1990 in Albuquerque, New Mexico.

Cassandra Margarita Rodriguez
(Cassandra Margarita Rodriguez)

The forgoing instrument, consisting of four pages, including this witness page, was declared, signed, and published by Cassandra Margarita Rodriguez as her Last Will and Testament in the presence of us, who were all present at the same time, and who, in her presence and at her request, have signed our names as witnesses. We declare that to the best of our knowledge, she appeared to be of legal age, of sound mind and memory, and under no constraint or undue influence at the time she executed the foregoing instrument. We declare this to be true under penalty of perjury.

Joseph Brown, 5432 Edmunds Place, Albuquerque, NM
Francis Bober, 345 Concord Avenue, Albuquerque, NM
Lauren Shea, 9807 Arizona Place, Albuquerque, NM

Sample Pour-Over Will

A pour-over will allows you to pass some or all of your property to an existing revocable living trust. In this will, Gail names her husband as guardian of their child, makes a few general gifts of money, and instructs that her residuary estate be transferred over to a revocable living trust she and her husband created in March of 1989. Whatever property is accounted for in Gail's will has to be probated before it can be transferred to her beneficiaries and to her living trust.

Last Will and Testament of Gail Lazaroff

I, Gail Lazaroff, a resident of Los Angeles County in Los Angeles, California, being of sound mind and memory and not acting under any duress, fraud or undue influence, declare this to be my Last Will and Testament.

1. I revoke all previous wills and codicils made by me.

2. I am married to Robert Lazaroff, herein referred to as my husband, and together we have one child, Jake Lazaroff, born July 8, 1990. It is my intention that my will include the above named child and any other children born to or adopted by me after the date of this will.

3. If any of my children are still minors at the time of my death, I nominate my husband to serve as guardian over their person and property. If he does not or cannot serve for any reason, I nominate my sister, Theresa Kelly for the position. No guardian shall be required to furnish bond.

4. No beneficiary in my will shall be deemed to have survived me unless living on the 30th day after my death.

Continued on Following Page

5. I make the following general gifts of money:

I give the sum of $5,000 to my niece Catherine Waller to be used in any way she wants, if she survives me, or if not, I direct that the sum of $5,000 become a part of my residuary estate and be distributed accordingly.

I give the sum of $5,000 to my nephew Jeffrey Waller to be used in any way he wants if he survives me, or if not, I direct that the sum of 5,000 become a part of my residuary estate and be distributed accordingly.

6. I give the residue of my estate, whether real or personal and wherever situated, to the Gail Lazaroff and Robert Lazaroff Revocable Living Trust dated March 17, 1989.

7. I nominate my husband to serve as the executor of my estate. If he does not or cannot serve for any reason, I nominate my sister, Theresa Kelly for the position. Any appointed executor shall not be required to post a bond.

8. My executor shall have the authority to perform any act he or she thinks necessary and in the best interest of my estate and descendants, with no limitations, and consistent with the laws of California. In addition, my executor is authorized to:

a. retain, until distribution and without liability for loss or depreciation resulting from such retention, any of my assets which shall come into his or her possession as a result of administering my estate.

b. mortgage, lease, pledge, exchange, partition, or sell any of my assets without prior court order, whether real or personal, at public or private sale and to invest or reinvest the proceeds from any sale in the best interest of my estate.

c. pass any real or personal property which is encumbered by a mortgage, deed of trust, lease or any other loan obligation that requires the payment of money, to the recipient of that particular property.

d. exercise or sell any or all conversion, subscription, option, voting and other rights of whatsoever nature pertaining to any such property, and in their discretion to vote, in person or by proxy, with respect to any matters regarding stocks, securities or other assets constituting part of my estate.

Continued on Following Page

e. retain and continue to operate any business, incorporated or otherwise, which is a part of my estate, including the right to effectuate any plan of corporate or business reorganization, consolidation, merger or similar plan.

f. prosecute, compromise, settle or submit to arbitration any claim in favor or against my estate.

g. appoint and pay a reasonable compensation to any agent, representative or attorney hired to handle any matter concerning my estate.

h. settle my estate without intervention of any court, except to the extent required by law.

9. I direct that my executor pay all estate, inheritance and other taxes assessed against my estate, including assets passing under or outside of my will, out of my residuary estate.

IN WITNESS WHEREOF I have signed this Will on this 11th day of May, 1990, in Los Angeles, California.

Gail Lazaroff
(Gail Lazaroff)

The forgoing instrument, consisting of three pages, including this witness page, was declared, signed and published by Gail Lazaroff as her Last Will and Testament in the presence of us, who were all present at the same time, and who, in her presence and at her request, have signed our names as witnesses. We declare that to the best of our knowledge, she appears to be of legal age, of sound mind and memory and under no constraint or undue influence at the time she executed the foregoing instrument. We declare this to be true under penalty of perjury.

Rhonda Watts, 2 Kenyon Street, Los Angeles, California
David Bell, 55 Fordham Road, Pasadena, California
Barbara Alford, 398 Walnut Street, Los Angeles, California

Appendix V:

SAMPLE
LIVING WILL

Everyone should draft a living will as a part of their estate plan. This appendix includes a "general" living will that can be used by residents of every state and the District of Columbia.

If you become seriously ill or injured, unable to communicate, and haven't made your wishes known about what kind of medical treatment you want or expect, health-care decisions could be made on your behalf that you don't agree with. In particular, you could be kept artificially alive by today's modern life-support systems — indefinitely.

A living will is a written document that instructs your doctor(s) and family members not to prolong your life by using artificial life-support systems, but instead to allow you to die a "natural" death. The sample below also includes an optional *proxy* clause that allows you to name someone who can make sure your wishes are heard and carried out. For example, if you're treated in a hospital that does not recognize living wills (even though your state may recognize living wills, not all hospitals do), your proxy can make sure you are transferred to a hospital that honors living wills.

For more information about living wills and a free state-specific form and instructions, contact *Choice In Dying*, a non-profit membership organization dedicated to educating health-care professionals and the public about "end-of-life" decisions and issues. Their address is 200 Varick Street, New York, NY 10014.

ADVANCE DIRECTIVE
Living Will and Health Care Proxy

Death is a part of life. It is a reality like birth, growth and aging. I am using this advance directive to convey my wishes about medical care to my doctors and other people looking after me at the end of my life. It is called an advance directive because it gives instructions in advance about what I want to happen to me in the future. It expresses my wishes about medical treatment that might keep me alive. I want this to be legally binding.

If I cannot make or communicate decisions about my medical care, those around me should rely on this document for instructions about measures that could keep me alive.

I do not want medical treatment (including feeding and water by tube) that will keep me alive if:

- I am unconscious and there is no reasonable prospect that I will ever be conscious again (even if I am not going to die soon in my medical condition), or
- I am near death from an illness or injury with no reasonable prospect of recovery.

I do want medicine and other care to make me more comfortable and to take care of pain and suffering. I want this even if the pain medicine makes me die sooner.

I want to give some extra instructions. *[Here list any special instructions, e.g., some people fear being kept alive after a debilitating stroke. If you have wishes about this, or any other conditions, please write them here.]*

The legal language in the box that follows is a health care proxy.
It gives another person the power to make medical decisions for me.

I name _____
who lives at _____
phone number _____ to make medical
decisions for me if I cannot make them myself. This
person is called a health care "surrogate," "agent,"
"proxy," or "attorney in fact." This power of attorney shall
become effective when I become incapable of making or
communicating decisions about my medical care. This
means that this document stays legal when and if I lose
the power to speak for myself, for instance, if I am in a
coma or have Alzheimer's disease.

My health care proxy has the power to tell others what my
advance directive means. This person also has the
power to make decisions for me, based either on what I
would have wanted, or, if this is not known, on what he or
she thinks is best for me.

If my first choice health care proxy cannot or decides not
to act for me, I name _____
address _____
phone number _____ as my second
choice.

I have discussed my wishes with my health care proxy, and
with my second choice if I have chosen to appoint a
second person. My proxy(ies) has (have) agreed to act for
me.

I have thought about this advance directive carefully. I
know what it means and want to sign it. I have chosen two
witnesses, neither of whom is a member of my family, nor
will inherit from me when I die. My witnesses are not the
same people as those I named as my health care proxies. I
understand that this should be notarized if I use the box to
name (a) health care proxy(ies).

_____
Signature

_____
Date

_____
Address

_____
Witness' Signature

_____

Witness' Printed Name

_____

Address

_____

Witness' Signature

_____

Witness' Printed Name

_____

Address

_____

Notary [to be used if proxy is appointed]

Reprinted by permission of Choice In Dying (formerly Concern for Dying/Society for the Right to Die).

Appendix VI:

GLOSSARY

The following terms are used in this book. Italicized terms in definitions are themselves defined in other glossary entries.

ADMINISTRATOR – Person or corporation appointed by the court to settle the estate (i.e. pay taxes, bills and distribute property to *heirs*) of a deceased person if no valid *will* can be found. See also *personal representative.*

AFFIDAVIT – Written statement of fact voluntarily signed and sworn to before a person having authority to administer an oath.

ASSETS – Money and *real* or *personal property* owned by a person or organization.

ATTESTATION CLAUSE – The clause found after the *testator's* signature on a will which contains the statement of the *witnesses* and their signatures.

BENEFICIARY– Person who is named to receive some benefit or money from a legal document such as a *will*, life insurance policy, or *trust.*

BEQUEST – Gift of *personal* or *real property* left in a *will.*

CODICIL – A document that revises the provisions of an existing *will.*

COMMUNITY PROPERTY – Property acquired during marriage that was not a *gift* to or inheritance of one spouse or specifically kept separate.

CREDIT ESTATE TAX – State tax on the assets of someone who has died. Applies only in some states and only to estates that are required to pay federal estate taxes. Estate does not pay double taxes but instead, by paying a credit estate tax, "rebates" part of the federal estate tax owed back to the state.

CREDITOR – Person or corporation to whom money is owed.

DEATH TAX – Another name for *inheritance* and *estate tax.*

DECEDENT – Person who has died.

DEVISE – Gift of *real property* left in a *will.*

DISINHERIT – Preventing a person from inheriting property under a *will.*

DURABLE POWER OF ATTORNEY – A legal document whereby one person authorizes another to make medical and financial decisions should illness or incapacitation occur.

ESTATE – All property, *real* or *personal*, that a person owns.

ESTATE TAX – A type of *death tax* based on the *decedent's* right to transfer property; not a tax on the property itself.

EXECUTOR – Person or corporation appointed in a *will* or by a court to settle the *estate* of a deceased person (female gender, *executrix*).

FEDERAL ESTATE TAX – Federal tax assessed against the *assets* of a person who has died if the value of the taxable assets exceed $600,000.

GIFT – A voluntary lifetime or at-death transfer of property, made without compensation.

GIFT TAX – A tax on lifetime transfers of property given without consideration or for less consideration than the property is worth.

GROSS ESTATE – Property owned by a *decedent* at death.

GUARDIAN – Person or corporation appointed by a court to handle the affairs or property of another who is unable to do so because of age or incapacity.

HEIR – Any person who inherits, or is entitled under law to inherit, property from a deceased person.

INCOME – All financial gains from investments, work, or business.

INHERITANCE TAX – A tax imposed on property received by *beneficiaries* from the *estate* of a *decedent*.

INTESTATE – Not leaving a valid *will.*

INVENTORY – Detailed accounting of articles of property with their estimated value, required by the court to settle most cases.

ISSUE – Offspring descended from a common ancestor (children, grandchildren, great-grandchildren, etc.).

IRREVOCABLE TRUST – A *trust* that cannot be changed or canceled after it is created.

JOINT TENANCY WITH RIGHT OF SURVIVORSHIP – Form of ownership in which property is equally shared by all owners and is automatically transferred to the surviving owners when one of them dies.

LEGACY — Gift of money left in a *will.*

LIVING (OR INTER VIVOS) TRUST – A *trust* that is set up and put into effect while the person who created the trust is living.

LIVING WILL – A document in which a person, while competent to do so, expresses a wish that his or her life not be prolonged by artificial life-support systems if his or her medical condition becomes hopeless.

PER CAPITA – A distribution plan that requires that a deceased *beneficiary's* share of a *testator's* estate be divided equally among the remaining named beneficiaries or if the testator wants, among all living descendants.

PERSONAL PROPERTY – Property that is moveable, not land or things attached to land.

PERSONAL REPRESENTATIVE – Person named in a *will* or appointed by a court to settle an *estate.*; also called PR. See also *executor.*

PER STIRPES – A distribution plan that requires that descendants of a deceased *beneficiary*, as a group, inherit equal shares of the amount the deceased beneficiary would have received had he or she lived. (For example, if your child predeceases you, any grandchildren descended from that child would receive equal shares of your deceased child's inheritance.)

PRINCIPAL – The property in a *trust*.

PROBATE – Legal process of establishing the validity of a deceased person's last will and testament; commonly refers to the process and laws for settling an *estate*.

PROXY – Someone who is authorized to act for another; an agent.

REAL PROPERTY – Property that's immovable, such as land, buildings and whatever else is attached to or growing on land.

RESIDUARY ESTATE – That part of the *estate* remaining after specific *bequests* have been made.

REVOCABLE TRUST – A *trust* that can be taken back, canceled, or changed.

SELF-PROVED WILL – A *will* accepted by the probate court as valid without further verification by witnesses.

SURETY BOND – A monetary guarantee that, should an executor mismanage or steal from an estate, compensation will be awarded up to the bond's limit.

SURVIVORSHIP CLAUSE – A will clause that determines how long a named *beneficiary* must live after the *testator's* death to inherit under the *will*.

TENANCY BY ENTIRETY – Form of spousal ownership in which property is equally shared and automatically transferred to the surviving spouse. While both spouses are living, ownership of the property can be altered only by divorce or mutual agreement.

TENANCY IN COMMON – A way of jointly owning property in which each person's share passes to his or her *heirs* or *beneficiaries,* but the ownership shares need not be equal.

TESTAMENTARY TRUST – A *trust* established in a person's *will*.

TESTATE – Dying with a valid *will*.

TESTATOR – Person who draws up a *will*.

TITLE – Ownership of property, or the document that shows ownership.

TRUST – Real or personal property held by one party (the *trustee*) for the benefit of another (the *beneficiary*).

TRUSTEE – Person who holds and/or manages money or property for the benefit of another.

UNLIMITED MARITAL DEDUCTION – The unlimited marital deduction allows a spouse to transfer all property to his or her spouse without federal *estate tax*.

WILL – Legal document that declares how a person wishes property to be distributed to *heirs* or *beneficiaries* after death.

WILL CONTEST – Challenge of a *will* by a person who believes the will is unfair or that one or more of its provisions does not accurately reflect how the deceased person wanted his or her property distributed.

WITNESS – Person who is present at an event or the signing of a document such as a *will.*

Appendix VII:

BIBLIOGRAPHY

All-States Wills and Estate Planning Guide: Basic Principles and a Summary of State and Territorial Will and Intestacy Statutes, Section of General Practice, American Bar Association, 750 North Lake Shore Dr., Chicago, IL 60611. 1990. 437 pages. $69.95.

> *This book serves as a tool for lawyers who write wills. Includes sample will clauses, "state-specific" forms for self-proving affidavits and statutory requirements for all 50 states, the District of Columbia, Puerto Rico, Virgin Islands, and Guam.*

The Complete Guide to Living Wills, by Evan R. Collins, Jr. and Doron Weber. Bantam Books, 666 5th Ave., New York, NY 10103. 1991. 323 pages. $9.50.

> *Discusses the primary reasons for creating a living will. Includes examples of living wills and durable powers of attorney, glossary and state-by-state guide with do-it-yourself forms.*

The Complete Will Kit, by Jens C. Appel III, and F. Bruce Gentry. John Wiley & Sons, Inc., 605 3rd Ave., New York, NY 10158-0012. 1990. 210 pages. $17.95.

> *A "do-it-yourself" book that helps you write a legally valid will in all 50 states and the District of Columbia. Includes tear-out, fill-in-the blank will forms and tips on selecting executors and updating wills.*

*The Essential Guide To a Living Will: How To
    Protect Your Right To Refuse Medical
    Treatment*, by B. D. Colen. Prentice Hall, Inc.,
    15 Columbus Cir., New York, NY 10023. 1991.
    146 pages. $7.95.
      *Explains the role of doctors and modern
      technology, writing your living will, and
      preparing a videotaped living will.*

Estate Planning Made Simple, by Merle E. Dowd.
    Doubleday, 666 5th Ave., New York, NY 10103.
    1991. 176 pages. $11.00.
      *Explores numerous estate-planning options,
      including wills, trusts, gift giving, probate-
      avoidance techniques, insurance and more.
      Includes glossary.*

How to Make A Will – How to Use Trusts, by
    Parnell Callahan. Oceana Publications, Inc., 75
    Main St., Dobbs Ferry, NY 10522. 1992. 200
    pages. $17.50.
      *Part of Oceana's "Legal Almanac Series," this
      book provides a clause-by-clause explanation
      of wills and useful information on trusts.*

*How to Use Trusts to Avoid Probate & Taxes: A
    Guide to Living, Marital, Support, Charitable
    and Insurance Trusts,* by Theresa Meehan
    Rudy, Kay Ostberg & Jean Dimeo in association
    with HALT. Random House, 201 E. 50th St.,
    New York, NY 10022. 1992. 231 pages. $10.00.
    (Available from HALT.)
      *As the title suggests, this book provides a
      complete overview of trusts. Information on
      "living" and "testamentary" trusts, the pros and
      cons of each and how to get a trust drafted.
      State-by-state appendices, tax charts and
      glossary are included.*

Introduction to Estate Planning, by Chris J.
   Prestopino. Kendall-Hunt, 2460 Kerper Blvd.,
   Dubuque, IA 52001. 1992. 640 pages. $44.95.
      *A recently updated textbook. Author gives an
      overview of estate planning concepts and tax
      information and illustrates specific strategies
      with examples and charts. Includes an extensive
      glossary.*

*The Jacoby & Meyers Law Offices Guide to Wills
   and Estates*, by Gail J. Koff, Esq. Henry Holt and
   Co., Inc., 115 W. 18th St., New York, NY 10011.
   1991. 88 pages. $4.95.
      *A brief guide covering will basics. Also includes
      information on will contests, taxes and
      handwritten (holographic) wills.*

*Leaving Money Wisely: Creative Estate Planning
   for Middle and Upper-Income Americans for
   the 1990's*, by David W. Berlin. Charles
   Scribner's Sons, 866 3rd Ave., New York, NY
   10022. 1990. 325 pages. $19.95.
      *The focus is on different estate-planning
      strategies for transfering property, lowering
      taxes, and avoiding probate. Includes sample
      wills and trusts.*

Making A Will and Creating Estate Plans, by
   Harvey J. Platt. Longmeadow Press, 201 High
   Ridge Rd., Stamford, CT 06904. 1991. 101 pages.
   $4.95.
      *A brief guide that explains and defines wills,
      probate and trusts. Discusses taxes and
      planning strategies. Includes glossary.*

Plan Your Estate With A Living Trust: Wills, Probate Avoidance and Taxes, by Denis Clifford. Nolo Press, 950 Parker St., Berkeley, CA 94710. 1991 (National Ed.). 416 pages. $19.95.

A recently updated plain-language discussion of estate planning. Topics include wills, the role of trusts in estate planning, making gifts, reducing your tax liability, planning for incapacitation, and more. Includes sample will and revocable living trust forms.

The Power of Attorney Book, by Denis Clifford. Nolo Press, 950 Parker St., Berkeley, CA 94710. 1991 (4th Ed.). 320 pages. $19.95.

This book contains forms and instructions for creating your own conventional or durable power of attorney, as well as advice on when and how to delegate authority over your health, financial and personal affairs.

Prepare Your Own Will: The National Will Kit, by Daniel Sitarz. Nova Publishing Co., 1103 W. College St., Carbondale, IL 62901. 1991 (3rd Ed.). 240 pages. $15.95.

A "do-it-yourself" will preparation kit that allows individuals and married couples to draft wills with, or without, children's trusts. Also lets you draft a living will and includes general information about estate planning.

Probate – Settling an Estate: A Step-by-Step Guide, by Kay Ostberg in association with HALT. Random House, 201 E. 50th St., New York, NY 10022. 1990. 162 pages. $8.95. (Available from HALT.)

A "how-to" book for handling probate from start to finish. Includes a list of probate rules and death-tax rates for each state and a check list of the tasks that need to be done.

Simple Will Book, by Denis Clifford. Nolo Press, 950 Parker St., Berkeley, CA 94710. 1990 (2nd Ed.). 256 pages. $17.95.
Enables U.S. residents (except in Louisiana) to write their own legally valid will. Tips on selecting an executor, filling out property inventory forms, leaving property to children in trust, and more.

Thy Will be Done: A Guide to Wills, Taxation and Estate Planning for Older Persons, by Eugene J. Daly. Prometheus Books, 700 E. Amherst St., Buffalo, NY 14215. 1990. 230 pages. $15.95.
A four-part book that discusses wills, probate, taxes and "final thoughts" on estate planning. Offers sample situations and money-saving suggestions for each section. Includes glossary and a "simple" will.

The Way of Wills: Trust and Estate Planning for Government Employees, by G. Jerry Shaw, Thomas J. O'Rourke and Virginia Hurt Johnson. MPC Publications, 715 8th St., SE, Ste. 300, Washington, DC 20003. 1990. 120 pages. $10.00.
Explains how to plan your estate using wills, trusts and probate avoidance techniques. Written specifically for federal workers; includes glossary.

Legal Software
Please check local book stores and software stores for the most up-to-date computer programs available.

Home Lawyer, by Hyatt Legal Services and MECA Ventures, Inc., 327 Riverside Ave., Westport, CT 06880. 1990. $89.90.
IBM computer program creates simple wills for individuals or married couple (execpt for Louisiana). Trust provisions not included. Over a dozen other legal documents available, including powers of attorney, promissory notes, and rental agreements.

It's Legal, by Parsons Technology, Inc.,1 Parsons Drive., P.O. Box 100, Hiawatha, IA 52233.1991. $29.00.
IBM compatible software, written by attorneys, helps you to prepare simple wills (except in Louisiana), living wills, leases, powers of attorney, certificates of guardianship, and promissory notes. Comes with user manual.

Personal Lawyer, by Bloc Publishing Co., 800 S.W. 37th Ave., Ste. 765, Coral Gables, FL 33134. 1992. $50.00.
IBM compatible software of five do-it-yourself forms: will, power of attorney, statement of guardianship, promissory note, and lease. Question-and-answer format to complete user's personalized form. Not valid for wills in Louisiana.

WillMaker, by Legisoft. Nolo Press, 950 Parker St., Berkeley, CA 94710. 1990 (4th Ed.). $69.95.
A Macintosh- and IBM-compatible program. This software lets non-lawyers create a will in every state except Louisiana. Also helps you prepare testamentary trusts for people who can't handle their money (spendthrifts), disadvantaged people, and for groups of beneficiaries.